C000039587

EYEWITNESS TRAVEL GUIDES

JAPANESE
PHRASE BOOK

A Dorling Kindersley Book

Dorling **DK** Kindersley

LONDON, NEW YORK, MUNICH,
MELBOURNE, AND DELHI

Compiled by Lexus Ltd with Keiko Holmes and Anthony P Newell

First American Edition 1999

Published in the United States by DK Publishing, Inc.
375 Hudson Street, New York, New York 10014

Reprinted with corrections 2000, 2003
10

019-ED125-Mar/03

DK Publishing offers special discounts for bulk purchases for sales promotions or
premiums. Specific, large-quantity needs can be met with special editions, including
personalized covers, excerpts of existing guides, and corporate imprints. For more
information, contact Special Markets Department, DK Publishing, Inc.,
375 Hudson Street, New York, NY 10014 Fax: 212-689-5254.

Library of Congress Cataloging-in-Publication Data
Japanese phrase book / by Lexus Ltd. with Keiko Holmes and
Anthony P. Newell.
   p.   cm. -- (Dorling Kindersley travel guides phrase books)
   ISBN-13: 978-0-7894-9490-0 (alk. paper)
   1. Japanese language--Conversation and phrase books--English.
I. Holmes, Keiko.   II. Newell, Anthony P.   III. Lexus (Firm)
IV. Series.
PL539.J38 1999
495.6'83421--dc21   98–53864
                                                                   CIP
Printed and bound in China by Leo Paper Products Limited

see our complete catalog at
www.dk.com

Picture Credits

Jacket photography: COINS; NATIONAL BANK

CONTENTS

PREFACE

This *DK Eyewitness Travel Guide Phrase Book* has been compiled by experts to meet the general needs of tourists and business travelers. Arranged under headings such as Hotels, Driving, and so forth, the Japanese words and phrases you may need to use are printed in a modified version of the standard system of romanization—the way in which Japanese characters are written in our alphabet. Detailed guidance on pronunciation is given on page 6.

Most sections of this book include boxes headed *Things You'll See*, which list the common words, signs, notices, etc. that you may see in Japanese characters. The boxes headed *Things You'll Hear* contain typical replies to questions you may ask.

A 2,000-line mini-dictionary will help you form additional phrases (or at least express the one word you need), and the extensive menu guide will ease your way through complicated Japanese meals. Under the heading Cross-Cultural Notes, you will find information on aspects of the Japanese way of life—points of etiquette, good manners, and customs. An understanding of such matters will greatly enhance your trip to Japan, and your hosts will appreciate all the effort you have made to respect their culture and speak their language.

DK Eyewitness Travel Guides are recognized as the world's best travel guides. Each title features specially commissioned color photographs, cutaways of major buildings, 3-D aerial views, and detailed maps, plus information on sights, events, hotels, restaurants, shopping, and entertainment.

PRONUNCIATION

When reading the imitated pronunciation, the same value should be given to all syllables as there is practically no stress in Japanese words (say **Yo-ko-ha-ma** and not **Yo-ho-HAR-ma**). Pronounce each syllable as if it formed part of an English word and you will be understood sufficiently well. Remember the points below and your pronunciation will be even closer to the correct Japanese.

a   as in "Ma" but shorter
e   as in "bed"
i   as the vowel sound in "leaf"
o   as in "more" but shorter
u   as in "put"

A bar-line over a vowel means that the vowel should be spoken with twice the length of a single vowel. When two vowels come together, be careful to give each one its proper individual sound:

ai   as in "wine"
ae   as if written "mah-eh"
ei   as if written "ay"

There are no silent letters, so don't forget to pronounce every one, including the **e** at the end of a word (**mame** is pronounced as if written **mah-meh**).

g   is hard as in "get"
j   as in "jet"

If a **p** or a **k** or another consonant, except for an **n**, comes at the end of a word, then it should be given its full value and not swallowed. Some systems write the word **kip**, for example, as **kip-pu**, which the authors of this book, however, consider an overemphasis on the value of the final sound.

CROSS-CULTURAL NOTES

Superficially, Japan can seem very Westernized with all its American movies, fast-food outlets, and Western-style hotels. But old habits die hard, and in Japan tradition is still strong. With some knowledge of Japanese customs and a bit of effort to accommodate what may seem strange, the visitor to Japan can show a feeling of respect and goodwill towards the Japanese people that will be amply rewarded.

When meeting a Japanese person for the first time, both bowing and shaking hands are common (sometimes even together). Many Japanese are now used to handshaking, but if you are being introduced to someone out of reach, or to a group of people, bowing is simpler: just bend slightly forward from the waist, nod your head, and smile.

Unless you are good friends, it is unusual to address a Japanese person by his or her first name. Stick to the surname and add **-san** (an all purpose word for Mr./Mrs./Ms.). From the Western point of view Japanese names are written backward, so, in **Tanaka Taro** "Tanaka" is the surname and "Taro" is the first name. The word **-san** can be added to first names as well as to surnames, but you should not use it when referring to yourself or when talking to members of your own family.

The Japanese people see themselves as a more or less classless society. But status is important, and in the business world, for example, you will find a rigid hierarchy in operation. If you in any way offend Japanese sensibilities, apologize profusely.

If you are invited to a Japanese home, removal of shoes is a must. Slippers will be offered at the **genkan**, or entrance. But even these must be left outside a room with **tatami** (straw matting). When you use the restroom you will usually find another pair of slippers there. Remember to change back out of your restroom slippers before reentering the other room!

When entering a room you can say **ojama-shi-mass**, which means literally, "I'm disturbing you," or **shitsurei-shi-mass**, which means literally, "I'm being impolite." The latter phrase can also be used when parting company.

Sometimes, when arriving at a Japanese home, you may be invited to take a bath. This is not a reflection of your host's opinion of your personal hygiene, but a courtesy offered to an honored visitor to enable him to relax. Remember: the bath is for relaxing; the shower is for washing. The bathroom floor is tiled, and it is on the floor that you wash yourself with soap and rinse off *before* stepping into the bath. The cardinal rule: don't get soap in the bathwater.

Some of the basic etiquette surrounding Japanese food and drink is:

- Be prepared to sit on cushions on the floor and use the damp cloth that will be offered to you to wipe your hands.

- Before eating, you thank your host with **itadaki-mass** (literally, "I receive"), and when finished, you again show your appreciation with **gochisō-sama deshta** (literally, "it was a feast").

- If you use chopsticks, never stand them upright in a bowl of rice (which is reminiscent of offerings to the dead). If you want to let go of them, place them on the chopstick rest provided or lay them flat on a bowl or plate. Chopsticks will often come joined at one end—just split them apart.

- Slurping noodles is quite acceptable.

- The way to eat soup is to hold the bowl to your mouth and drink. Some people also eat rice by holding the bowl to the mouth and shoveling the rice in using chopsticks.

- Don't pour soy sauce over your rice—pour it over your meat instead or into your side dish.

- Don't pour your own **sake**—pour someone else's, who will then reciprocate by filling your cup, which you should ideally hold while the drink is being poured.

Although hotels, restaurants, and department stores in big cities provide Western-style restrooms, Japanese-style restrooms are common (in trains, local inns, and many houses, for example). There are different sorts of Japanese-style toilet, but what they all have in common is the fact that they are not to be sat on. The user squats over the receptacle, facing the hood at the far end. It is advisable to carry your own supply of paper. Toilets are usually separate from bathrooms, so beware of asking for the bathroom if that's not exactly what you mean.

To the Japanese, the Western-style habit of blowing your nose into a handkerchief is an extremely distasteful practice. When you blow your nose, use a tissue. The Japanese use handkerchiefs for other purposes such as drying their hands when they have washed them after going to the restroom or as a napkin when eating.

If you see Japanese people wearing face masks, this does not mean they are concerned about breathing *in* polluted air, but rather that they have a cold and are anxious not to breathe *out* germs.

Western women visiting Japan should not find their treatment appreciably different from what they are used to at home. But if you are in Japan on business, wives will be noticeably absent from a company's social activities. If you are lucky enough to be invited home, the wife will probably retire to the kitchen after serving dinner. It is, however, typical in Japan for the wife to control the family budget and for the husband to bring his paycheck home and be given pocket money.

USEFUL EVERYDAY PHRASES

Yes/no
Hai/īe

Thank you
Dōmo arigatō

No, thank you
Kek-kō dess

Please *(offering)* Dōzo
(asking for something) Onegai-shi-mass

I don't understand
Wakari-masen

Do you speak English?
Eigo o hanashi-mass ka?

I can't speak Japanese
Nihongo wa hanase-masen

I don't know
Shiri-masen

Please speak more slowly
Mō skoshi yuk-kuri hanashte kudasai

Please write it down for me
Kaite kudasai?

My name is . . .
Watashi no namae wa . . . dess

How do you do, pleased to meet you
Hajime-mashte, dōzo yoroshku

Good morning
Ohayō gozai-mass

Good afternoon
Kon-nichi wa

Good evening
Kom-ban wa

Good night (*when going to bed*) Oyasumi nasai
(*when leaving a group early*) Osaki ni

Goodbye
Sayōnara

How are you?
Ogenki dess ka?

Excuse me, please
Shitsurei shi-mass

Sorry!
Sumi-masen

I'm really sorry
Hontō ni sumi-masen

Can you help me?
Chot-to sumi-masen

Can you tell me . . .?
. . . o oshiete kudasai?

May I have . . .?
. . . itadake-mass ka?

I would like . . .
. . . o itadake-mass ka?

Is there . . . here?
Koko ni . . . wa ari-mass ka?

Where can I get . . .?
. . . wa doko ni ari-mass ka?

How much is it?
Ikura dess ka?

What time is it?
Ima nanji dess ka?

I must go now
Mō ikanakereba nari-masen

I've lost my way
Michi ni mayot-te shimai-mashta

Cheers! (*toast*)
Kampai!

Do you take credit cards?
Kurejit-to kādo tskae-mass ka?

Where is the restroom?
Otearai wa doko dess ka?

Go away!
At-chi e it-te!

Excellent!
Sugoi!

I've lost my passport/money/room key/traveler's checks/ credit cards
Paspōto/kagi/toraberāz-chek/kurejit-to kādo o nakushmashta

Where is the US embassy?
Amerika taishkan wa dokodess ka?

THINGS YOU'LL HEAR

Abunai!	Look out!
Chot-to!	Hey!
Dō itashi-mashte	You're welcome
Dōmo	Thanks
Dōzo	Here you are
E? Nan dess ka?	Excuse me?
Genki dess, arigatō —anata wa?	Very well, thank you —and you?
Hajime-mashte, dōzo yoroshku	How do you do, nice to meet you
Ja mata	See you later
Ogenki dess ka?	How are you?
Sayonara	Goodbye
Sō dess	That's right
Sō dess ka?	Is that so?
Sumi-masen	Excuse me
Wakari-masen	I don't understand, I don't know

THINGS YOU'LL SEE

注意	**chūi**	caution
休日	**kyūjits**	closed
危険	**kiken**	danger
エレベーター	**erebētā**	elevator
非常口	**hijō-guchi**	emergency exit
入口	**iriguchi**	entrance
出口	**deguchi**	exit
案内	**an-nai**	information
男子用	**danshi-yō**	(for) men
立入禁止	**tachi-iri-kinshi**	no admittance
禁煙	**kin-en**	no smoking
開く	**hiraku**	open
営業中	**eigyō-chū**	open for business
故障	**koshō**	out of order
引く	**hiku**	pull
押す	**oss**	push
御手洗	**otearai**	restroom
閉じる	**tojiru**	shut
階	**-kai**	story, floor
女子用	**joshi-yō**	(for) women
化粧室	**keshō-shits**	women's restroom
円	**en**	yen

DAYS, MONTHS, SEASONS

Sunday	nichi-yōbi
Monday	getsu-yōbi
Tuesday	ka-yōbi
Wednesday	sui-yōbi
Thursday	moku-yōbi
Friday	kin-yōbi
Saturday	do-yōbi
January	ichi-gats
February	ni-gats
March	san-gats
April	shi-gats
May	go-gats
June	roku-gats
July	shchi-gats
August	hachi-gats
September	ku-gats
October	jū-gats
November	jū-ichi-gats
December	jū-ni-gats
Spring	haru
Summer	nats
Fall	aki
Winter	fuyu
Christmas	kuriss-mass
Christmas Eve	kuriss-mass ibu
New Year	oshō-gats
New Year's Eve	ō-misoka

THE CALENDAR

1st	tsuitachi
2nd	futska
3rd	mik-ka
4th	yok-ka
5th	itska
6th	muika
7th	nanoka
8th	yōka
9th	kokonoka
10th	tōka
11th	jū-ichi-nichi
12th	jū-ni-nichi
13th	jū-san-nichi
14th	jū-yok-ka
15th	jū-go-nichi
16th	jū-roku-nichi
17th	jū-shchi-nichi
18th	jū-hachi-nichi
19th	jū-ku-nichi
20th	hatska
21st	ni-jū-ichi-nichi
22nd	ni-jū-ni-nichi
23rd	ni-jū-san-nichi
24th	ni-jū-yok-ka
25th	ni-jū-go-nichi
26th	ni-jū-roku-nichi
27th	ni-jū-shchi-nichi
28th	ni-jū-hachi-nichi
29th	ni-jū-ku-nichi
30th	san-jū-nichi
31st	san-jū-ichi-nichi

NUMBERS

0	zero	○		10	jū	十
1	ichi	一		11	jū-ichi	十一
2	ni	二		12	jū-ni	十二
3	san	三		13	jū-san	十三
4	yon	四		14	jū-yon	十四
5	go	五		15	jū-go	十五
6	roku	六		16	jū-roku	十六
7	nana	七		17	jū-nana	十七
8	hachi	八		18	jū-hachi	十八
9	kyū	九		19	jū-kyū	十九

20	ni-jū	二十
21	ni-jū-ichi	二十一
22	ni-jū-ni	二十二
30	san-jū	三十
40	yon-jū	四十
50	go-jū	五十
60	roku-jū	六十
70	nana-jū	七十
80	hachi-jū	八十
90	kyū-jū	九十
100	hyaku	百
101	hyaku-ichi	百一

200	ni-hyaku	二百
300	sam-byaku	三百
400	yon-hyaku	四百
500	go-hyaku	五百
600	rop-pyaku	六百
700	nana-hyaku	七百
800	hap-pyaku	八百
900	kyū-kyaku	九百
1000	sen	千
2000	ni-sen	二千
3000	san-zen	三千
4000	yon-sen	四千
5000	go-sen	五千
6000	rok-sen	六千
7000	nana-sen	七千
8000	hass-sen	八千
9000	kyū-sen	九千
10,000	ichi-man	一万
20,000	ni-man	二万
100,000	jū-man	十万
200,000	ni-jū-man	二十万
1,000,000	hyaku-man	百万
2,000,000	ni-hyaku-man	二百万
10,000,000	sem-man	千万
20,000,000	ni-sem-man	二千万
100,000,000	ichi-ok	一億
123,456	jū-ni-man-san-zen- yon-hyaku-go-jū-rok	十二万三千 四百五十六

COUNTING

When counting *objects,* Japanese has different number words.
Note that the number comes after the object.

two beers	bīru futats

one	hitots
two	futats
three	mits
four	yots
five	itsuts
six	muts
seven	nanats
eight	yats
nine	kokonots
ten	tō

After ten, use the ordinary number words again. For counting
people, there are two special points to note:

one person	hito-ri
two people	futa-ri

After this, use **nin** with the ordinary number word:

three people	san-nin
ten people	jū-nin

TIME

today	kyō
yesterday	kinō
tomorrow	ashta
the day before yesterday	ototoi
the day after tomorrow	asat-te
this week	kon-shū
last week	sen-shū
next week	rai-shū
this morning	kesa
this afternoon	kyō no gogo
this evening	kom-ban
tonight	kon-ya
yesterday afternoon	kinō no gogo
last night	yūbe
tomorrow morning	ashta no asa
tomorrow night	ashta no ban
in three days	mik-ka go
three days ago	mik-ka mae
late	osoi
early	hayai
soon	sugu
later on	ato de
at the moment	ima
second	byō
minute	fun
one minute	ip-pun
two minutes	ni-fun
quarter of an hour	jū-go fun
half an hour	san-jup-pun
forty-five minutes	yon-jū-go-fun
hour	jikan
that day	sono hi
every day	mainichi
all day	ichi-nichi jū
the next day	sono yokujits ni

week (*this, last, next, etc.*)	-shū
(*one, two, three, etc.*)	shū-kan
fortnight	ni-shū-kan
month (*this, last, next, etc.*)	gets
(*one, two, three, etc.*)	kagets
this year	kotoshi
last year	kyonen
next year	rainen
one year	ichi-nen

TELLING TIME

In Japanese the hour comes first, followed by the minutes. If the minutes are "past" the hour, then just say the hour followed by the minutes, as when saying "five forty" or "six ten." So "five past two" is **ni-ji go-hun**. **Ji** means "hours" and **fun** means "minutes." If the minutes are "before" the hour, then the number of minutes plus **mae** (before) is used. So "five to three" is **san-ji go-fun mae**. The word for "half" is **han**, which is simply added to the hour (e.g., "half past three" is **san-ji han**). There is no special word for a quarter of an hour—just use fifteen minutes (**jū-go fun**). Timetables and other official lists use the twenty-four-hour clock written in Arabic numerals.

AM/PM	gozen/gogo
one o'clock	ichi-ji
ten past one	ichi-ji jup-pun
quarter past one	ichi-ji jū-go-fun
half past one	ichi-ji han
twenty to two	ni-ji ni-jup-pun mae
quarter to two	ni-ji jū-go-fun mae
two o'clock	ni-ji
16:30	jū-roku-ji san-jup-pun
at half past five	go-ji han ni
at seven o'clock	shchi-ji-ni
noon	shōgo
midnight	mayonaka

HOTELS

Advance reservations are generally recommended and can be made through the JTB (Japan Travel Bureau), whose offices can be found throughout Japan. There are two principal types of accommodations: Western-style hotels, **hoteru**, and Japanese-style inns, **ryokan**.

Hotels are comparable in range, cost, and quality with modern hotels in the US. Facilities and services are good, although the rooms are often smaller than their Western counterparts. Vending machines are found in most hotels for snacks, drinks, and certain basic items. Tipping is generally unnecessary (the exception being, perhaps, baggage porters) since a service charge of 10–15 percent will be levied. In addition, a 10 percent tax may be imposed, but only on bills exceeding a certain amount.

There are also what are known as "business hotels," or **bijiness hoteru**. These are found in urban centers and are aimed primarily at business people on a restricted budget. Consequently, they are very plain and offer a minimum amount of service.

Motels are relatively inexpensive, but it should be borne in mind that some motels are used as "love hotels."

Ryokan, which offer the traveler a real taste of the traditional Japanese lifestyle, are becoming increasingly popular among tourists. Staying at a **ryokan** is not necessarily less expensive than staying at a hotel, but the service is invariably excellent and the room charge customarily includes breakfast and dinner. Guests live on traditional **tatami** matting, sleep on a **futon**— Japanese bedding laid on the floor—eat Japanese cuisine, and can relax in a piping hot communal Japanese bath. The public baths are generally single sex, although there are still **ryokan** where men and women bathe together, particularly in the hot spring resorts of northern Japan, where people go expressly for the supposed therapeutic properties of the water. A number of **ryokan** have facilities for catering to Western visitors, providing, for example, individual baths for those Westerners of a shy disposition. Unlike the staff of Western-style hotels, those who run **ryokan** generally speak little or no English.

Four other types of accommodations are available:

Youth Hostels: Simple, neat, inexpensive, and usually well-sited, Japan's plentiful youth hostels are governed by the international rules of youth hosteling. A few are open to people of all ages, but many will require tourists to be members of their own national associations.

Minshku: Privately owned establishments, these are often run as sidelines by families who want to supplement their regular income, and they are the nearest Japanese equivalent to the bed and breakfast system. Rooms are simple (e.g., no luxury items like a refrigerator), the rates are very reasonable, and staying in a **minshku** will give you a good chance to try some real Japanese home cooking. Reservations (plus deposits) are required a month in advance.

Kokumin Shkusha (People's lodges): Allowing people a chance to enjoy inexpensive holiday accommodations in pleasant surroundings, these facilities are basically set up to meet the requirements of Japanese travelers on limited budgets. They bear a certain resemblance to rural **ryokan**, but are bigger and less expensive. Located away from urban centers, they are intended for vacationers rather than business people. As in the **ryokan**, little or no English can be expected.

Kokumin Kyūka-mura (National vacation villages): These are health resorts set in beautiful surroundings. There are facilities for outdoor recreation in addition to inexpensive accommodations. Foreign visitors will be expected to adopt a Japanese-like lifestyle.

USEFUL WORDS AND PHRASES

balcony	barukoni
bathroom	ofuroba
bed	bed-do
bedroom	heya
bill	seikyū-sho
breakfast	chōshok

dining room	shoku-dō
dinner	yūshok
double room	daburu
elevator	erebētā
full board	san-shoku-tski
half board	chōshok to yūshoku-tski
hotel	hoteru
key	kagi
lobby	robī
lounge	raunji
lunch	chūshok
manager	manējā
reception	huronto
receptionist	huronto no hito
restaurant	restoran
room	heya
room service	rūm-sābiss
shower	shawā
single room	shinguru
toilet	otearai
twin room	tsuin

Do you have any vacancies?
Heya ari-mass ka?

I have a reservation
Yoyak shte i-mass

I'd like a single/double/twin room
Shinguru/daburu/tsuin onegai-shi-mass

I'd like a room with a bathroom
Ofuro-tski no heya onegai-shi-mass

I'd like a room with a balcony
Barukonī-tski no heya onegai-shi-mass

I'd like a room for one night/three nights
Ip-pak/Sam-pak shitai dess

What is the charge per night?
Ip-paku ikura dess ka?

Is there satellite/cable TV in the rooms?
Heya ni eisei/kēbru terebi wa ari-mass ka?

Is there a highchair/crib/baby changing room?
Kodomo yō no isu/shōgiyō-shiudai/bebī rūm wa doko dess ka?

Is there wheelchair access?
Kuruma isu yō no tsūro wa ari-mass ka?

I don't yet know how long I'll stay
Nan-nichi tomaru ka mada wakari-masen

When is breakfast?
Chōshoku wa nanji dess ka?

When is dinner?
Yūshoku wa nanji dess ka?

Would you have my luggage brought up?
Nimotsu o mot-te kite kure-masen ka?

Please call me at . . . o'clock
. . . ji ni okoshte kudasai

May I have breakfast in my room?
Heya de chōshoku ha deki-mass ka?

I'll be back at . . . o'clock
. . . ji ni modori-mass

My room number is . . .
Watashi no heya wa . . . ban dess

I'm leaving tomorrow
Ashta tachi-mass

May I have the bill, please?
Seikyū-sho onegai-shi-mass?

I'll pay by credit card
Kurejit-to kādo de harai-mass

I'll pay cash
Genkin de harai-mass

Can you get me a taxi?
Takshī o yonde kure-masen ka?

Can you recommend another hotel?
Hoka ni ī hoteru ari-mass ka?

THINGS YOU'LL HEAR

Mōshi-wake gozai-masen ga ip-pai dess
I'm sorry, we're full

Shinguru wa fusagat-te ori-mass
There are no single rooms left

Daburu wa fusagat-te ori-mass
There are no double rooms left

Nan-paku dess ka?
For how many nights?

Oshi-harai wa dō nasai-mass ka?
How will you be paying?

→

Saki-barai de onegai-itashi-mass
Please pay in advance

Kono kādo ni kinyū shte itadake-mass ka?
Could you fill in this registration form, please?

Koko ni sain shte kudasai-mase
Sign here, please

Paspōto, omochi dess ka?
May I see your passport?

THINGS YOU'LL SEE

冷房	**reibō**	air-conditioning
バー	**bā**	bar
お風呂	**ofuro**	bath
食堂	**shokudō**	dining room
ダイニング・ルーム	**dainin-gu rūm**	dining room
飲み水	**nomi-mizu**	drinking water
飲料水	**inryō-sui**	drinking water
クリーニング	**kurīnin-gu**	dry cleaning
エレベーター	**erebētā**	elevator
非常口	**hijō-guchi**	emergency exit
消火器	**shōkaki**	fire extinguisher
一階	**ik-kai**	ground floor
暖房	**dambō**	heating
温泉	**onsen**	hot spring
ホテル	**hoteru**	hotel

→

日本交通公社	Nihon kōtsū kōsha	Japanese Travel Bureau
旅館	ryokan	Japanese-style inn
和室	washits	Japanese-style room
ロビー	robī	lobby
ラウンジ	raunji	lounge
男	otoko	men
立入禁止	tachi-iri-kinshi	no entry
民宿	minshku	people's inn
受付	uketske	reception
フロント	furonto	reception
レストラン	restoran	restaurant
お手洗い	otearai	restroom
室	heya	room
ルーム・サービス	rūm sābiss	room service
二階	ni-kai	second floor
自動販売機	jidō-hambai-ki	vending machine
洋室	yōshits	Western style room
女	on-na	women
ユース・ホステル	yūss-hosteru	youth hostel

DRIVING

There are plenty of car rental companies in Japan and comprehensive insurance is usually included in the rental charge. To rent a car you will need an international driver's license. In Japan, they drive on the *left* and road signs often follow international conventions, although signs giving names or information will be in Japanese. Gas is bought by the liter, and you may find that gas stations will also do certain minor repairs. A red triangle is essential and should be provided by the rental company. The JAF (Japan Automobile Federation) offers free assistance to foreigners in case of breakdown or emergency. Expressways or highways are good, but many ordinary roads are narrow and bumpy. In Japan you'll find that the roads are invariably overcrowded, a problem that is made worse by the lack of sidewalks, numerous train crossings, a lack of parking spaces, and ubiquitous electricity poles. All in all, driving in Japan can be a hazardous and frustrating experience.

USEFUL WORDS AND PHRASES

automatic	ōtomachik
brake (*noun*)	burēki
breakdown	koshō
car	kuruma
clutch	kuracchi
to drive	unten suru
engine	enjin
exhaust	haiki-gass
fanbelt	fam-beruto
garage (*for repairs*)	shūri-jo
gas	gasorin
gas station	gasorin-stando
gear(s)	giya
highway	kōsok-dōro
intersection	jū-ji-ro
junction (*on highway*)	intā

license	menkyo
license plate	nambā-purēto
lights (head)	hed-do-raito
(tail)	tēru-raito
manual (drive)	manyuaru
mirror	bak-mirā
motorcycle	ōtobai
road	michi
to skid	suberu
spare partss	speya
speed (noun)	sokudo
speed limit	sokudo-seigen
speedometer	sokudo-kei
steering wheel	handoru
tire	taiya
to tow	hiku
traffic lights	shingō
trailer	torērā
truck	torakku
trunk	torank
van	ban
wheel	sharin
windshield	uindo-skrĭn
windshield wiper	uindo-skrĭn waipā

I'd like some gas/oil/water
Gasorin/oiru/mizu onegai-shi-mass

Fill it up, please!
Mantan, onegai-shi-mass!

I'd like 10 liters of gas
Gasorin jū-rit-toru onegai-shi-mass

Would you check the tires, please?
Taiya o mite kure-masen ka?

Do you do repairs?
Shūri shte kure-masen ka?

Can you fix the clutch?
Kurachi naoshte kure-masen ka?

How long will it take?
Dono kurai kakari-mass ka?

Where can I park?
Doko ni chūsha deki-mass ka?

There is something wrong with the engine
Enjin ga okashii dess

The engine is overheating
Enjin ga obāhīto shi-mashta

I need a new tire
Atarashī taiya ga iri-mass

I'd like to rent a car
Kuruma o karitai no dess ga

Is there a mileage charge?
Kyori de harai-mass ka?

Can we rent a baby/child seat? (car seat)
Bebī shīto o karitai no dess ga?

Where is the nearest garage?
Ichiban chikai garēji wa doko dess ka?

How do I get to . . .?
. . . e, dō ikeba yoi dess ka?

Is this the road to . . .?
Kore na . . . e iku michi dess ka?

DIRECTIONS YOU MAY BE GIVEN

mass-sugu	straight ahead
hidari ni	on the left
hidari ni magaru	turn left
migi ni	on the right
migi ni magat-te	turn right
migi-gawa no saisho no michi	first on the right
hidari-gawa no nibam-me no michi	second on the left
. . . o tōt-te	past the . . .

THINGS YOU'LL HEAR

Ōtomachik ga ī dess ka, manyuaru ga ī dess ka?
Would you like an automatic or a manual?

Menkyo-shō o misete kudasai
May I see your license?

SOME COMMON ROAD SIGNS

この先100メートル	kono saki hyaku mētoru	100 meters ahead
この先100米	kono saki hyaku mētoru	100 meters ahead
事故	jiko	accident

→

自動車整備工場	jidōsha seibi kōjō	auto repairs
料金	ryōkin	charge
回り道	mawari-michi	detour
非常駐車帯	hijō chūsha-tai	emergency parking area
出口	deguchi	exit
高速道路	kōsok dōro	expressway
石油	sekiyu	gas
ガソリンスタンド	gasorin stando	gas station
交差点	kōsaten	junction
本線	honsen	lane for through traffic
最高速度	saikō sokudo	maximum speed
国道	kokudō	national highway
無料	mu-ryō	no charge
左折禁止	sasets kinshi	no left turn
駐車禁止	chūsha kinshi	no parking
右折禁止	usets kinshi	no right turn
停車禁止	teisha kinshi	no stopping
通行止	tsūkō-dome	no through traffic
通行禁止	tsūkō-kinshi	no through traffic
灯油	tōyu	paraffin
駐車場	chūsha-jō	parking lot
満車	man-sha	parking lot full

→

有料	yū-ryō	pay to park here
警察	keisats	police
スピード落せ	spĭdo otose	reduce speed
道路工事	dōrō-kōji	road under construction
工事中	kōji-chū	road work
急カーブ	kyū-kāb	sharp bend
一時預り	ichiji azukari	short-term parking
徐行	jokō	slow
止まれ	tomare	stop
一旦停車	it-tan tei-sha	stop
一旦停止	it-tan tei shi	stop
有料道路	yū-ryō dōro	toll road
踏切	fumi-kiri	train crossing

TRAIN TRAVEL

Japan runs a very efficient train system that is fast and punctual. Large stations offer all the usual services, including luggage porters (called **akabō** because of their red caps). First class coaches, "green cars," with a green four-leaf clover symbol on the side of the coach, offer roomy and comfortable reclining seats. Second class coaches are often crowded. Station names and important signs are given in both Japanese and English, although verbal announcements are always made in Japanese except on the "bullet train."

There are various categories of trains:

- **Shinkansen**: this is the "bullet train," one of the world's fastest luxury trains; there are three types – the **nozomi**, the **ikari**, and the **kodama**. The **nozomi** is the fastest, stopping only at major cities; the **kodama** stops at more stations than the **ikari** and therefore takes slightly longer to arrive.

- **Tok-kyū**: the special express that stops only at main stations.

- **Kyūkō**: the express, stopping more frequently than the **tok-kyū**.

- **Futsū**: the local train that stops at all stations.

There are plenty of automatic ticket-vending machines, but if in doubt you can always go to the ticket office. For the faster trains you pay an express surcharge; there is a further charge for reservations, but this is usually worthwhile since many trains are crowded.

Useful Words and Phrases

buffet	byuf-fe
car (of train)	kyak-sha
communication cord	hijō-tsūhō-sak
compartment	sha-shits
connection	norikae
dining car	shokudō-sha
engine	enjin
entrance	iriguchi
exit	deguchi
first class	it-tō
to get in	noru
to get out	oriru
guard	shashō
information board	hyōji-ban
lost and found	wasure-mono
luggage cart	te-oshi-guruma
luggage rack	nidai
luggage room	tenimotsu azukari-jo
luggage van	nimots-sha
one-way ticket	katamichi kip
platform	hōm
rail	rēru
railroad	tetsudō
reservation office	kip-pu uriba
reserved seat	shtei-seki
restaurant car	shokudō-sha
round-trip ticket	ōfuku kip
seat	seki
second class	ni-tō
sleeping car	shindai-sha
station	eki
station master	eki-chō
ticket	kippu
ticket collector	eki-in

timetable	jikok-hyō
tracks	rēru
train	densha
waiting room	machi-ai-shits
window	mado

When does the train for . . . leave?
. . . iki no densha wa nanji ni de-mass ka?

When does the train from . . . arrive?
. . . kara no densha wa nanji ni tski-mass ka?

When is the next train to . . .?
. . . yuki no tsugi no densha wa nanji dess ka?

When is the first train to . . .?
. . . yuki no saisho no densha wa nanji dess ka?

When is the last train to . . .?
. . . yuki no saigo no densha wa nanji dess ka?

What is the fare to . . .?
. . . made ikura dess ka?

Do I have to change?
Norikae nakereba nari-masen ka?

Does the train stop at . . .?
Densha wa . . . ni tomari-mass ka?

How long does it take to get to . . .?
. . . made dono kurai kakari-mass ka?

A one-way/round-trip ticket to . . ., please
. . . made katamichi/ōfuku ichi mai onegai-shi-mass

Do I have to pay a supplement?
Tsuika-kin o harawa-nakereba nari-masen ka?

I'd like to reserve a seat
Seki o yoyak shtain dess

Is there a family ticket available?
Kazoku ken wa ari-mass ka?

Is there a reduction for children?
Kodomo ryōkin wa arimass ka?

Is this the right train for . . .?
. . . e wa kono densha de in dess ka?

Is this the right platform for the . . . train?
. . . densha wa kono hōm de in dess ka?

Which platform for the . . . train?
. . . densha wa dono hōm dess ka?

Is the train late?
Densha wa okurete-i-mass ka?

Could you help me with my luggage, please?
Nimotsu o mot-te kure-masen ka?

Is this a nonsmoking compartment?
Kore wa kin-en-sha dess ka?

Is this seat free?
Kono seki wa aite-i-mass ka?

This seat is taken
Kono seki wa aite-i-masen

I have reserved this seat
Kono seki o yoyak shte-i-mass

May I open the window?
Mado o akete mo ī dess ka?

May I close the window?
Mado o shimete mo ī dess ka?

When do we arrive in . . .?
. . . ni nanji ni tski-mass ka?

What station is this?
Koko wa doko eki dess ka?

Do we stop at . . .?
. . . ni tomari-mass ka?

Is there a dining car on this train?
Kono densha ni shokudō-sha wa ari-mass ka?

THINGS YOU'LL HEAR

Gorenku itashi-mass
Attention

Kip-pu o haiken sasete itadaki-mass
Tickets, please

Chot-to sumi-masen!
Excuse me!

Ori-mass!
I'm getting off!

Tsumete kudasai!
Move along, please!

THINGS YOU'LL SEE

特急	tok-kyū	(abbreviation for) limited express
大人	otona	adult
前売券	mae-uri-ken	advance sale tickets
下車前途無効	gesha zento mukō	after getting off, not valid for futher travel
到着	tōchak	arrival(s)
荷物	nimots	baggage
コインロッカー	koin rok-kā	baggage locker
一時預り所	ichiji-azukari-jo	baggage storage
のりば・乗り場	noriba	boarding platform
回数券	kaisū-ken	book of tickets
…行き	. . . yuki	bound for . . .
新幹線	shinkan-sen	bullet train
三号車	san-gō-sha	car no. 3
小人・子供	kodomo	child
出発	shup-pats	departure(s)
発車	hash-sha	departure(s)
行先	yuki-saki	destination
食堂車	shokudō-sha	dining car
方面	hōmen	direction
東口	higashi guchi	east exit

→

精算所	seisan-jo	excess fare office
急行	kyūkō	express
一等	it-tō	first class
みどりの窓口	midori-no-madoguchi	first class ticket window
200円区間ゆき	ni-hyaku-en kukan yuki	for destinations within the 200-yen zone
グリーン車	gurīn-sha	green car
団体	dantai	group
車掌	shashō	guard
個人	kojin	individual
JR	jay aru	Japan Railways
左側通行	hidari gawa tsūkō	keep to the left
右側通行	migi gawa tsūkō	keep to the right
売店	baiten	news agent
特別急行	tokubets-kyūkō	limited express
…線	. . . sen	. . . line
お忘れもの	oswasure-mono	lost and found
お忘れもの承り所	oswasure-mono uketa-mawari-jo	lost and found office
地図	chizu	map
次	tsugi	next

→

北口	**kita guchi**	north exit
無効	**mukō**	not valid
普通	**futsū**	ordinary
ホーム	**hōm**	platform
入場券	**nyū-jō-ken**	platform ticket
私鉄	**shitets**	private railroads
鉄道	**tetsudō**	railroad
指定席（券）	**shtei-seki (-ken)**	reserved seat (ticket)
定期券	**teiki-ken**	season ticket
席	**seki**	seat
座席	**zaseki**	seat
二等	**ni-tō**	second class
準急	**jun-kyū**	semi-express
南口	**minami guchi**	south exit
駅	**eki**	station
駅長	**eki-chō**	station master
地下鉄	**chikatets**	subway
料金表	**ryōkin-hyō**	table of charges
運賃表	**unchin-hyō**	table of fares
乗換口	**nori-kae-guchi**	this way for changing trains
切符	**kip**	ticket
…券	**. . .-ken**	. . . ticket

→

改札口	kai-sats guchi	ticket barrier
きっぷうりば 切符売場	kip-pu uriba	ticket office/ machine
窓口	madoguchi	ticket window
出札口	shuss-sats-guchi	ticket window
時刻表	jikok-hyō	timetable
二番線	ni-ban-sen	track no. 2
電車	densha	train
列車	resh-sha	train
自由席	ji-yū-seki	unreserved seat
有効	yūkō	valid
発売当日限り有効	hatsubai tōjits kagiri yūkō	valid only on day of purchase
経由	keiyu	via
待合室	machi-ai-shits	waiting room
西口	nishi guchi	west exit

AIR TRAVEL

Inquiries should be made at the Japanese embassy in the country of departure for details on visas, customs formalities, and vaccination requirements. This done, entry formalities can be kept to a minimum, requiring the filling-in of a disembarkation form on the plane, a stamp in your passport from the immigration officer, and perhaps a **nani mo arimasen**—I have nothing (to declare)—from you to the customs officer. Many airport officials can speak at least some English, and all major airports have very good information centers staffed by English-speaking people.

USEFUL WORDS AND PHRASES

aircraft	hikōki
airline	kōkū
airport	kūkō
airport shuttle	eyapōto bass
aisle	tsūro
arrival	tōchak
baggage claim	onimotsu uketori-jo
boarding pass	tōjō-ken
check-in (*noun*)	chek-ku-in
check-in desk	chek-ku-in kauntā
customs	zeikan
delay	okure
departure	shup-pats
departure lounge	shup-pats raunji
emergency exit	hijō guchi
flight	hikō
flight attendant (*male*)	schūwādo
(*female*)	schūwādess
flight number	furaito bangō
gate	gēto
jet	jet-to

to land	chaku-rik suru
long-distance flight	chōkyori bin
passport	paspōto
passport control	nyūkok shinsa
pilot	pairot-to
runway	kas-sō-ro
seat	seki
seat belt	shīto-beruto
takeoff	ririk
window	mado
wing	tsubasa

When is there a flight to . . .?
. . . iki no huraito wa its dess ka?

What time does the flight to . . . leave?
. . . iki no huraito wa nanji ni shup-pats shi-mass ka?

Is it a direct flight?
Chok-kō-bin dess ka?

Do I have to change planes?
Norikae nakereba nari-masen ka?

When do I have to check in?
Chek-ku-in wa nanji dess ka?

I'd like a one-way ticket to . . .
. . . iki no katamichi onegai-shi-mass

I'd like a round trip ticket to . . .
. . . iki no ōfuku onegai-shi-mass

I'd like a nonsmoking seat, please
Kin-en seki onegai-shi-mass

I'd like a smoking seat, please
Kitsuen no hō onegai-shi-mass

I'd like a window seat, please
Madogawa onegai-shi-mass

How long will the flight be delayed?
Hikōki wa dono kurai okure-mass ka?

Is this the right gate for the . . . flight?
. . . yuki no furaito no gēto wa koko dess ka?

Which gate for the flight to . . .?
. . . yuki no furaito no gēto wa doko dess ka?

When do we arrive in . . .?
. . . ni nanji ni tski-mass ka?

May I smoke now?
Ima tabako o sut-te mo ī dess ka?

I do not feel very well
Kibun ga yoku ari-masen

THINGS YOU'LL HEAR

Tadaima kara . . . bin no tōjō tetsuzuki o hajime-mass
The flight for . . . is now boarding

. . . ban gēto ni onarabi kudasai
Please go now to gate number . . .

THINGS YOU'LL SEE

航空	**kōkū**	airline
航空券	**kōkū-ken**	airline ticket
空港	**kūkō**	airport
全日空	**Zen Nik-kū**	All Nippon Airways
到着	**tōchak**	arrivals
搭乗券	**tōjō-ken**	boarding pass
バス	**bass**	buses
税関	**zeikan**	customs
出発	**shup-pats**	departures
国内線	**kokunai-sen**	domestic airlines
免税店	**menzei-ten**	duty-free shop
搭乗口	**tōjō-guchi**	gate
ゲート	**gēto**	gate
出入国管理	**shuts-nyū-koku kanri**	immigration
御案内所	**go-an-nai jo**	information desk
国際線	**koksai-sen**	international airlines
日本航空	**Nihon Kōkū**	Japan Airlines
予約	**yoyak**	reservations
タクシー	**takshi**	taxis
東亜国内航空	**Tōa Kokunai Kōkū**	TOA Domestic Airlines

BY BUS, TAXI, AND SUBWAY

Buses abound, but in the rush hour they are slow and over-crowded. In general, they are less convenient than trains unless you know where to get off. Different systems operate: sometimes you board at the front and exit at the rear; sometimes it's the other way around. Sometimes you pay for the distance traveled; sometimes there is a flat fare. Whatever the fare is, you usually drop it into the "farebox" or **ryōkim-bako** rather than hand it to the driver. No English can be expected from either bus signs or bus drivers.

Taxis can be flagged down in the street (a red light indicates an available cab) or you can line up at a taxi stand **takshī noriba**. Try to have the address you want to go to written down in Japanese. Preferably, this should be accompanied by a map since addresses in Japan are notoriously difficult to find. Many streets have no name and the numbering system has a form of logic unique to Japan. For the return trip, just hand the driver one of your hotel's business cards (available at the front desk). Always get in and out of the taxi on the left—and don't try to open the door by yourself: this is done automatically by a gadget operated by the driver. A late night surcharge is in effect between 11:00 PM and 5:00 AM. Tipping is not required.

There are subways, **chikatets** in large cities like Tokyo, Osaka, Kyoto, and Sapporo. With the dense congestion on Japan's roads, the subway is often the fastest and most reliable means of transportation. Fares depend on the distance traveled, and tickets are most conveniently obtained from vending machines (which also give change). During the rush hour, stations both above and below ground are only for those of a strong and healthy disposition.

Other means of transportation: there are many ferries around Japan, plus a few trams in big cities (though these are fast disappearing). There is a monorail from downtown Tokyo to Haneda Airport. Ask for details at a JTB office. Do not expect to find rickshaws.

Useful Words and Phrases

adult	otona
boat	bōto
bus	bass
bus stop	bass-tei
child	kodomo
connection	renraku
driver	untenshu
fare	ryōkin
ferry	ferī
long-distance bus	chōkyori-bass
number 5 bus	go-ban no bass
passenger	jōkyak
port	minato
river	kawa
rush hour	rash-shu-awā
seat	seki
station	eki
subway	chikatets
terminal	shūten
ticket	kip
tram	shigai-densha
transit system map	chizu

Where is the nearest subway station?
Moyori no chikatets no eki wa doko dess ka?

Where is the bus station?
Bass no eki wa doko dess ka?

Where is there a bus stop?
Bass-tei wa doko dess ka?

Which buses go to . . .?
Dono bass ga . . . e iki-mass ka?

How often do the buses to . . . run?
. . . iki no bass wa ichi-jikan ni nambon ari-mass ka?

Would you tell me when we get to . . .?
. . . ni tsuitara oshiete kure-masen ka?

Do I have to get off yet?
Mada ori-naktemo in dess ka?

How do you get to . . .?
. . . e wa dō iki-mass ka?

Is it very far?
Totemo tōi dess ka?

I want to go to . . .
. . . e ikitai to omoi-mass

Do you go near . . .?
. . . no chikaku e iki-mass ka?

Where can I buy a ticket?
Doko de kip ga kae-mass ka?

Do we have to pay for the children?
Kodomo no bun mo shiharau no dess ka?

Could you close the window?
Mado o shimete kure-masen ka?

Could you open the window?
Mado o akete kure-masen ka?

Could you help me get a ticket?
Kip-pu o kau no o tetsudat-te kure-masen ka?

When does the last bus leave?
Saishū bass wa nanji ni de-mass ka?

THINGS YOU'LL SEE

自動ドア	jidō-doa	automatic door
バス	bass	bus
バス乗り場	bass-noriba	bus boarding point
バス停	bass-tei	bus stop
バスターミナル	bass-tāminaru	bus terminal
乗車は前扉から	jōsha wa mae-tobira kara	enter at front door
降車は後扉から	kōsha wa ushiro-tobira kara	exit at rear door
料金箱	ryōkim-bako	fare box
運賃箱	unchim-bako	fare box
料金メーター	ryōkin-mētā	fare meter
空車	kūsha	for rent
駅前	eki-mae	in front of station
夜間割増し料金	yakan warimashi ryōkin	late night fare
回送	kaisō	out of service
次停車	tsugi teisha	stopping at next stop
地下鉄	chikatets	subway
タクシー	takshĭ	taxi
タクシー乗り場	takshĭ-noriba	taxi stand

51

DOING BUSINESS

Position within a hierarchy is important to the Japanese. Your business card, which is a crucial item to take, should state what your position is within your own company or the Japanese will be confused. Foreign businessmen often make the mistake of addressing the wrong level of authority within a Japanese company. Key figures will be the **buchō** (department or division chief) and the **kachō** (section chief). The **kachō** makes all the routine business decisions and supervises their implementation. Do not attempt to bypass such people and go straight to the top.

The foreign businessman looking for a quick decision will most likely be frustrated in Japan. A key concept in Japanese business is that of **nemawashi**—the groundwork prior to decision-making involving enlisting the support of all those concerned in the decision-making process. It should also be appreciated that the Japanese approach to a business decision is less along the lines of "what's in it for us?" or "what's the profit?" than "what are we getting ourselves into?" Strategic issues of market share tend to override tactical considerations of quick profit. First meetings should be seen as an occasion for establishing "face" and for triggering groundwork.

Although Japanese men do not tend to regard women as equals, foreign businesswomen will be given "honorary male" status.

Here are some tips that might make your trip more successful: It is a good idea to take small gifts for your Japanese business partners. If you are taken out for a meal, do not insist on paying. Bowing is no longer essential in Japan—shaking hands is quite acceptable. Learn something about Japanese customs (see page 7). Learn some facts about Japan: the names of the prime minister and foreign minister, the names of the governor of the Bank of Japan and the president of the company you're dealing with, even the names of some movie stars or sports heroes. In other words, show some interest in and knowledge of Japan. Those who ignore such basics will find themselves in Japan climbing not just a hill but a very steep mountain.

Useful Words and Phrases

accept	shōdak suru
accountant	keiri-shi
accounts department	keiri-ka
advertisment	kōkok
advertising	kōkoku-gyō
to air freight	eya-fureito
bid	nyūsats
to bill	seikyū-sho o tskuru
board (of directors)	jūyaku-kai
brochure	pan-furet-to
business card	meishi
businessman	bijinesman
chairman	kaichō
client	okyak-san
company	kaisha
computer	kompyūtā
consumer	shōhi-sha
contract	keiyak
cost	genka
customer	okyak-san
director	direktā
discount	waribiki
documents	shorui
down payment	atama-kin
engineer	gishi
executive	egzekutib
expensive	takai
exports	yushuts-hin
fax	faks
inexpensive	yasui
to import	yunyū suru
imports	yunyū-hin
installment	bunkats-barai
invoice	seikyū-sho
letter	tegami

letter of credit	shin-yō-jō
loss	sonshits
manager	manējā
manufacture	seizō suru
margin	baibai-saeki
market	shijō
marketing	māke-tin-gu
meeting	kaigi
modem	modem
negotiations	kōshō
offer	mōshide
order	chūmon
to order	chūmon suru
personnel	jinji
photocopier	kopī ki
price	nedan
product	seihin
production	seisan
profit	rieki
promotion (*publicity*)	hanbai-sokushin
purchase order	kai-chūmon
sales department	hambai-ka
sales director	hambai-buchō
sales figures	uriage
secretary	hisho
shipment	funazumi
tax	zeikin
telex	tereks
tender	nyūsats
total	gōkei

My name is . . .
Watashi no namae wa . . . dess

Here's my card
Meishi o dōzo

Pleased to meet you
Dōzo yoroshku onegai-shi-mass

May I introduce . . .?
. . . o goshōkai itashi-mass

My company is . . .
Watashi no kaisha wa . . . dess

Our product is selling very well in the US market
Waga-sha no seihin wa Amerika no shijō de hijō ni yoku urete
ori-mass

We are looking for partners in Japan
Waga-sha de wa Nihon de no pātonā o motomete ori-mass

At our last meeting . . .
Sempan no uchiawase de wa . . .

10 percent/25 percent/50 percent
Jup-pāsento/ni-jū-go-pāsento/go-jup-pāsento

More than . . .
. . . ijō

Less than . . .
. . . ika

What's your fax number/email address?
Fakks bangō/denshi meiru no jūsho o oshiete kudasai?

Did you get my fax/email?
Watashi no fakks/denshi meiru o uketorimashta ka?

Can I send an email/fax from here?
Koko kara denshi meiru/fakks o okure mass ka?

We're on schedule
Yotei dōri dess

We're slightly behind schedule
Yotei yori skoshi okurete i-mass

Please accept our apologies
Mōshi-wake gozai-masen

There are good government grants available
Seifu no hojo ga ari-mass

It's a deal
Kore de yoroshī dess ne

I'll have to check that with my chairman
Kaichō to sōdan shte o-henji shi-mass

I'll get back to you on that
Sono koto wa ato de o-henji shi-mass

You will have our quote very shortly
Dekiru dake hayaku mitsumori o sashiage-mass

We'll send it by telex
Terek-ksu itashi-mass

We'll send them air freight
Eya-fureito de okurasete itadaki-mass

It's a pleasure to do business with you
Otak to torihiki deki-mashte ureshku omoi-mass

We look forward to a mutually beneficial business relationship
Dōzo yoroshku onegai-itashi-mass

EATING OUT

Japan offers a wealth of eating and drinking places with an amazing variety of cuisines. Many restaurants specialize in a certain type of food, so check before you go in. Menus with prices are often displayed in the window together with very realistic plastic or wax replicas of the food offered, enabling you to point to what you want to order.

In traditional Japanese-style restaurants, you will have to remove your shoes and sit on floor cushions. If you are in a group, you can reserve an **ozashki**, a private dining room. Chopsticks are usually used for Asian food, but knives and forks are always available on request. Western-style food is also widely available, especially in hotels and big department stores (usually on the top floor). Japanese tea usually comes free, together with **oshibori**, a damp cloth to wipe your hands and face with. Fixed-price lunches, **teishok** or **ranchi**, are very popular and generally a good value for the money. Special portions are available for children, **okosama ranchi**. For notes on etiquette, see the Cross-Cultural Notes section. Tipping is usually unnecessary since the bill will include a service charge.

For snacks you'll find plenty of street stalls, snackbars, hamburger and pizza restaurants, and fried chicken shops. For drinking there are numerous coffee shops and bars (though beware of hostess bars where huge bills get run up in no time at all). In the summer many department stores open beer gardens on the roof. Japanese beer comes in several varieties, most of which taste like German lager. The traditional drink of Japan is, of course, **sake**, brewed from fermented rice and often served hot.

Useful Words and Phrases

beer	bīru
bottle	bin
bowl	chawan
cake	kēki
check	okanjō

chef	kok
chopsticks	hashi
coffee	kōhī
cup	kap
fork	fōk
glass	gurass
knife	naif
menu	menyū
napkin	napkin
plate	osara
receipt	ryōshū-shō
sandwich	sandoichi
snack	keishok
soup	sūp
spoon	spūn
sugar	osatō
table	tēburu
tea (*Japanese*)	ocha
(*Western*)	kōcha
teaspoon	tīspūn
tip	chip
waiter	uētā
waitress	uētoress
water	mizu
(*iced*)	ohiya
wine	wain
wine list	wain risto

A table for one/two, please
Hitori/Futari onegai-shi-mass

May I see the menu?
Menyū onegai-shi-mass

May I see the wine list?
Wain risto onegai-shi-mass

What would you recommend?
Nani ga osusume dess ka?

I'd like . . .
Watashi wa . . . ga ī dess

May I have one of those?
Sore o hitotsu onegai-shi-mass?

Just a cup of coffee, please
Kōhī ip-pai dake onegai-shi-mass

Waiter/waitress!
Chot-to sumi-masen!

May we have the check, please?
Okanjō onegai-shi-mass?

I only want a snack
Keishok de īn dess

Is there a fixed-price menu?
Teishoku wa ari-mass ka?

Is this suitable for vegetarians?
Kore wa bejitarian demo dai jōbu dess ka?

I'm allergic to nuts/shellfish
Watashi wa nattsu/kai arerugī desu

I didn't order this
Kore wa chūmon shi-masen deshta

May we have some more . . .?
Mot-to . . . onegai-shi-mass?

Can you warm this bottle/baby food for me?
Kono honyū bin/bebĭ fūdo o atatamete kudasai?

The meal was very good, thank you
Gochisō-sama deshta, totemo oish-kat-ta dess

PLACES TO EAT

きっさてん・喫茶店	kiss-saten	coffee shop
けいしょくきっさ 軽食喫茶	keishoku-kiss-sa	coffee shop serving light meals
りょうてい・料亭、 かっぽう・割烹	ryōtei, kap-pō	expensive, quality restaurant
のみや・飲み屋、 いざかや・居酒屋	nomiya, izakaya	local bar
レストラン、 しょくどう・食堂、 りょうりや・料理屋	restoran, shokudō, ryōriya	restaurant
こりょうりや 小料理屋、 めしや・飯屋	koryōriya, meshiya	small local restaurant
スナック けいしょく・軽食 スナックバー	snak, keishok, snakbā	snack bar
しょうじんりょうりや 精進料理屋	shōjin ryōriya	vegetarian restaurant
しょくじどころ 食事所	shokujidokoro	very small local restaurant

MENU GUIDE

APPETIZERS AND SOUPS

ハム	**ham**	ham
オードブル	**ōdōburu**	hors d'oeuvres
おつまみ・お撮み	**otsumami**	Japanese-style appetizer
つきだし・突き出し	**tskidashi**	Japanese-style appetizer
いせえび・伊勢海老	**ise-ebi**	lobster
メロン	**meron**	melon
ミネストローネ	**minestorōne**	minestrone
マッシュルームの ポタージュ	**mashrūm no potaj**	mushroom soup
くるまえび・車海老	**kuruma-ebi**	prawns/jumbo shrimp
スモークサーモン	**smōk sāmon**	smoked salmon
みそしる・味噌汁	**misoshiru**	soup with bean paste
トマトスープ	**tomato sūp**	tomato soup

EGG DISHES

ベーコンエッグ	**bēkon-eg**	bacon and eggs
たまご・卵	**tamago**	egg
めだまやき・目玉焼き	**medama-yaki**	fried eggs
ハムエッグ	**hamu-eg**	ham and eggs

たまごやき・卵焼き	**tamago-yaki**	Japanese-style omelette
オムレツ	**omurets**	omelette
オムライス	**omuraiss**	omelette with rice
ちゃわんむし 茶碗蒸し	**chawam-mushi**	seasoned "custard" with egg and fish
たまごどうふ 卵豆腐	**tamago-dōhu**	steamed egg and bean curd

FISH AND SUSHI

あわび	**awabi**	abalone
すずき	**suzuki**	bass
ふぐ	**fugu**	blowfish
かつお	**katsuo**	bonito, tuna
うな重	**unajū**	broiled eel on rice
うなどん・うな丼	**unadon**	broiled eel on rice
こい	**koi**	carp
はまぐり	**hamaguri**	clam
たら	**tara**	cod
たらこ	**tarako**	cod roe
あなご	**anago**	conger eel
かに	**kani**	crab
うなぎ	**unagi**	eel
上	**jō**	expensive selection
並	**nami**	inexpensive selection

にしん	**nishin**	herring
かずのこ	**kazunoko**	herring roe
あじ	**aji**	horse mackerel
さば	**saba**	mackerel
五目寿司	**gomoku-zushi**	mixed "sushi"
散らし寿司	**chirashi-zushi**	mixed "sushi" on rice
たこ	**tako**	octopus
おしずし	**oshi-zushi**	Osaka-style "sushi" cut in squares
かき	**kaki**	oyster
さしみ	**sashimi**	raw fish
すし	**sushi**	raw fish on rice balls
にぎりずし	**nigiri-zushi**	raw fish on rice balls
さけ	**sake**	salmon
いくら	**ikura**	salmon roe
いわし	**iwashi**	sardines
帆立て貝	**hotategai**	scallop
たい	**tai**	sea bream
かっぱまき	**kap-pa-maki**	seasoned rice and cucumber wrapped in seaweed
いなりずし	**inari-zushi**	seasoned rice wrapped in fried "tofu"
うに	**uni**	sea urchin
えび	**ebi**	shrimp

のりまき	**nori-maki**	sliced roll of rice, vegetables, and fish powder, wrapped in seaweed
いか	**ika**	squid
あゆ	**ayu**	sweet smelt
ます	**mass**	trout
まぐろ	**maguro**	tuna
鯨	**kujira**	whale
ぶり	**buri**	yellowtail

MEAT AND POULTRY

バーベキュー	**bābekyū**	barbecue
ぎゅうにく・牛肉	**gyūnik**	beef
ビーフ	**bĭf**	beef
てっぱんやき 鉄板焼	**tep-panyaki**	beef and vegetables grilled at the table
ぎゅうしょうがやき 牛生姜焼	**gyūshōgayaki**	beef cooked in soy sauce with ginger
ビフテキ	**bihuteki**	beef steak
くしやき・串焼	**kushiyaki**	broiled meat on skewers
にわとり	**niwatori**	chicken
あばらにく・肋肉	**abaranik**	chops
コロッケ	**korok-ke**	croquettes

とんかつ・豚カツ	**tonkats**	deep-fried pork cutlets
カツどん・カツ丼	**katsudon**	deep-fried pork on rice
あひる	**ahiru**	duck
ヒレにく・ヒレ肉	**hirenik**	fillet
やきにく・焼肉	**yakinik**	fried pork marinated in soy sauce
ハンバーグ	**hambāg**	hamburger
レバー	**rebā**	liver
にく・肉	**nik**	meat
にくだんご・肉団子	**nikudango**	meat-filled dumplings
ほねつき・骨付き	**honetski**	on the bone
ぶたにく・豚肉	**butanik**	pork
ぶたしょうがやき 豚生姜焼	**butashōgayaki**	pork cooked in soy sauce with ginger
うずら	**uzura**	quail
カレーライス	**karēraiss**	rice with curry-flavored stew
ローストビーフ	**rōstobǐf**	roast beef
ローストチキン	**rōsto chikin**	roast chicken
ローストポーク	**rōsto pōk**	roast pork
ソーセージ	**sōsēji**	sausage
サーロイン	**sāroin**	sirloin

やきとり・焼き鳥	**yakitori**	skewered fowl cooked over a grill
しゃぶしゃぶ	**shabu-shabu**	sliced beef with vegetables boiled at the table
すきやき・すき焼	**skiyaki**	sliced beef with vegetables cooked at the table
スペアリブ	**speyarib**	spareribs
すずめ	**suzume**	sparrow
ステーキ	**stēki**	steak

RICE DISHES

…どんぶり・…丼	**. . . domburi**	bowl of rice with something on top
うなぎどんぶり	**unagi domburi**	"domburi" with broiled eel
おやこどんぶり 親子丼	**oyako domburi**	"domburi" with chicken and egg
てんどん・天丼	**tendon**	"domburi" with deep-fried shrimps
たまごどんぶり 卵丼	**tamago domburi**	"domburi" with onions cooked in egg
ちゅうかどんぶり 中華丼	**chūka domburi**	"domburi" with pork and vegetables
にくどん・肉丼	**nikudon**	"domburi" with sliced beef

カツどん・カツ丼	**katsudon**	"domburi" with deep-fried breaded pork cutlet
チャーハン	**chāhan**	fried rice
ごはん・御飯	**gohan**	rice
ライス	**raiss**	rice
かまめし・釜飯	**kamameshi**	rice steamed in fish bouillon with pieces of meat, fish, and vegetables
チキンライス	**chikin raiss**	rice with chicken
おにぎり	**onigiri**	rice balls wrapped in seaweed

VEGETABLES, SEASONINGS, AND SALADS

アスパラ	**aspara**	asparagus
竹の子	**takenoko**	bamboo shoots
とうふ	**tōfu**	bean curd
豆	**mame**	beans
おひたし	**ohitashi**	boiled spinach with seasoning
キャベツ	**kyabets**	cabbage
にんじん	**ninjin**	carrot
コーン	**kōn**	corn
きゅうり	**kyūri**	cucumber
なす	**nass**	eggplant

みそ	miso	fermented soybean paste
なっとう	nat-tō	fermented soybeans
油揚げ	abura-age	fried bean curd
しょうが	shōga	ginger
ピーマン	pǐman	green pepper
まつたけ	mats-take	Japanese mushrooms
のり	nori	kind of seaweed
レタス	retass	lettuce
マヨネーズ	mayonēz	mayonnaise
マッシュルーム	mashrūm	mushrooms
きのこ	kinoko	mushrooms (general term)
からし	karashi	mustard
あぶら・油	abura	oil
玉ねぎ	tamanegi	onion
ポテト	poteto	potatoes
ポテトサラダ	poteto-sarada	potato salad
サラダ	sarada	salad
塩	shio	salt
からい・辛い	karai	salty
しょうゆ・醬油	shōyu	soy sauce
大豆	daizu	soybeans
ほうれん草	hōrensō	spinach

おさとう・お砂糖	osatō	sugar
あまい・甘い	amai	sweet
トマト	tomato	tomato
野菜	yasai	vegetables
す・酢	su	vinegar
たくあん	takuan	yellow radish pickles

FRUITS AND NUTS

バナナ	banana	banana
さくらんぼ・桜ん坊	sakurambo	cherries
くり・栗	kuri	chestnuts
ココナッツ	kokonats	coconut
くだもの・果物	kudamono	fruit
フルーツ	furuts	fruit
グレープフルーツ	gurēp-fūrūts	grapefruit
レモン	remon	lemon
メロン	meron	melon
オレンジ	orenji	orange
もも・桃	momo	peach
かき・柿	kaki	persimmon
みかん・蜜柑	mikan	tangerine
くるみ・胡桃	kurumi	walnuts
すいか・西瓜	suika	watermelon

DESSERTS

アップルパイ	**ap-puru pai**	apple pie
ケーキ	**kēki**	cake
チーズケーキ	**chǐz-kēki**	cheesecake
チョコレート	**chokorēto**	chocolate
シュークリーム	**shūkurǐm**	cream puff
うじごおり・宇治氷	**uji gōri**	crushed ice with green tea syrup
氷メロン	**kōri meron**	crushed ice with melon syrup
デザート	**dezāto**	dessert
ドーナッツ	**dōnats**	doughnut
ゼリー	**zerǐ**	gelatin
みつまめ・密豆	**mitsumame**	gelatin cubes and sweet beans with pieces of fruit
アイスクリーム	**aiskurǐm**	ice cream
パイナップル	**painap-puru**	pineapple
パインヨーグルト	**pa-in yōguruto**	pineapple yogurt
きいちご	**kǐchigo**	raspberry
おもち・お餅	**omochi**	rice cakes
おせんべい	**osembei**	rice crackers
まんじゅう・饅頭	**manjū**	riceflour cakes with bean jam

シャーベット	**shābet-to**	sorbet
ショートケーキ	**shōto kēki**	shortcake
ようかん・羊かん	**yōkan**	soft, sweet bean paste
スフレ	**sufure**	soufflé
カステラ	**kastera**	sponge cake
いちご・苺	**ichigo**	strawberries
ストロベリー アイスクリーム	**storoberī aiskurīm**	strawberry ice cream
おしるこ・お汁粉	**oshiruko**	sweet bean soup with rice cake
プリン	**purin**	vanilla egg custard with brown sugar
バニラアイスクリーム	**banira aiskurīm**	vanilla ice cream
クリームあんみつ	**kurīmu am-mits**	vanilla ice cream on gelatin cubes, served with sweet beans and fruit
ヨーグルト	**yōguruto**	yogurt

NOODLE DISHES

ラーメン・拉麺	**rāmen**	Chinese noodles
チャーシューメン	**chāshūmen**	Chinese noodles in pork bouillon
チャンポン	**champon**	Chinese noodles in salted bouillon with vegetables

カントンメン・広東麺	kantom-men	Chinese noodles in salted pork-flavored soup with vegetables
そば・蕎麦	soba	long, brownish buck-wheat noodles
うどん・饂飩	udon	long, thick, white, wheat flour noodles
そうめん・素麺	sōmen	long, thin, white, wheat flour noodles
ワンタンメン・饂飩麺	wantam-men	noodle-like squares containing ground pork and leeks, served in soup with noodles
やきそば・焼そば	yaki soba	noodles (griddle-fried) with small pieces of vegetable and meat
てんぷらそば 天麩羅蕎麦	tempura soba	noodles in fish bouillon with deep-fried shrimp
つきみそば・月見蕎麦	tskimi soba	noodles in fish bouillon with raw egg on top
にくなんばん・肉南蛮	niku namban	noodles in fish bouillon with pork or beef

かけそば・掛蕎麦	kake soba	simple dish of noodles in fish broth
きつねうどん・狐饂飩	kitsune udon	noodles in fish broth with fried bean curd
ちからうどん・力饂飩	chikara udon	noodles in fish broth with rice cake
もやしそば・萌そば	moyashi soba	noodles in pork broth with bean sprouts
もりそば・盛り蕎麦	mori soba	noodles served cold, to be dipped into sweetened soy sauce
みそラーメン 味噌ラーメン	miso rāmen	noodles and pork in bean paste broth
ごもくそば・五目そば	gomok soba	"soba" in broth with pieces of vegetable and meat

JAPANESE-STYLE FIXED PRICE MEALS

定食	teishok	meal with rice, soup, pickles, and main dish
ひがわりていしょく 日変り定食	higawari teishok	"teishok" of the day
てんぷらていしょく 天麩羅定食	yakiniku teishok	"teishok" with broiled meat as the main dish

やきにくていしょく 焼肉定食	**tempura teishok**	"teishok" with deep-fried shrimp as the main dish
とんかつていしょく 豚カツ定食	**tonkats teishok**	"teishok" with pork as the main dish
さしみていしょく 刺身定食	**sashimi teishok**	"teishok" with raw fish as the main dish
おひるのていしょく 御昼の定食	**ohiru no teishok**	lunchtime "teishok"
べんとう・弁当	**bentō**	boxed lunch (sold at train stations)

SNACKS

パン	**pan**	bread
バター	**batā**	butter
チーズロール	**chĭzurōru**	cheese on a roll
フライドチキン	**furaido chikin**	fried chicken
ハムサンド	**hamusando**	ham sandwich
ジャム	**jam**	jam
ランチ	**ranchi**	lunch
マーマレード	**māmarēdo**	marmalade
ピザ	**piza**	pizza
サンドイッチ	**sandoichi**	sandwich
スパゲッティ	**spaget-ti**	spaghetti
トースト	**tōsto**	toast

CHINESE MEALS

すぶた・酢豚	**subuta**	a kind of sweet and sour pork
マーボーどうふ マーボー豆腐	**mābō-dōfu**	bean curd in spicy soup mixture
ちゅうかりょうり 中華料理	**Chūka ryōri**	Chinese food
はるまき・春巻	**harumaki**	egg roll, deep-fried
ギョーザ・餃子	**gyōza**	fried dumplings stuffed with ground pork
くらげのすのもの 海月の酢物	**kurage no sunomono**	sliced parboiled jellyfish
シューマイ・焼売	**shūmai**	small steamed pork dumplings in thin Chinese pastry

CULINARY CATEGORIES AND METHODS OF PREPARATION

のみもの・飲み物	**nomimono**	beverages
ろばたやき・炉端焼	**robatayaki**	charcoal-grilled fish and vegetables
ちゅうかりょうり 中華料理	**Chūka ryōri**	Chinese-style cuisine
お菓子	**okashi**	confectionery
かっぽう・割烹	**kap-pō**	customer-requested Japanese-style cordon bleu dishes
あげもの・揚げ物	**agemono**	deep-fried foods

てんぷら・天麩羅	**tempura**	deep-fried seafood and vegetables in batter
あえもの・和え物	**aemono**	dressed foods (salads)
なべもの・鍋物	**nabemono**	food cooked in a pot at the table
やきもの・焼物	**yakimono**	grilled or broiled foods
かいせきりょうり 懐石料理	**kaiseki ryōri**	Japanese haute cuisine
にほんりょうり 日本料理	**Nihon ryōri**	Japanese-style cuisine
めんるい・麺類	**menrui**	noodle dishes
つけもの・漬け物	**tskemono**	pickled foods
とりりょうり・鳥料理	**tori-ryōri**	poultry dishes
きょうどりょうり 郷土料理	**kyōdo ryōri**	regional specialties
ごはんもの・御飯物	**goham-mono**	rice dishes
にもの・煮物	**nimono**	simmered foods
しるもの・汁物	**shirumono**	soups
むしもの・蒸し物	**mushimono**	steamed foods
しょうじんりょうり 精進料理	**shōjin ryōri**	vegetarian cuisine
すのもの・酢の物	**sunomono**	vinegary foods
せいようりょうり 西洋料理	**seiyō ryōri**	Western-style cuisine

DRINKS

ビール	**bǐru**	beer
紅茶	**kōcha**	black tea
ココア	**kokoa**	cocoa
コーヒー	**kōhǐ**	coffee
コーラー	**kōrā**	cola
しょうちゅう・焼酎	**shōchū**	distilled rice spirit
なまビール・生ビール	**nama bǐru**	draft beer
ソーダー水	**sōdā sui**	green, sweet soda
お茶	**ocha**	Japanese tea
レモンティ	**remon tǐ**	lemon tea
ミルク	**miruk**	milk
ぎゅうにゅう・牛乳	**gyūnyū**	milk
ミルクセーキ	**miruk sēki**	milk shake
ミネラル ウォーター	**mineraru uōtā**	mineral water
オレンジ ジュース	**orenji jūss**	orange juice
オレンジスカッシュ	**orenji skash**	orange (juice) drink
パイン ジュース	**pa-in jūss**	pineapple juice
さけ・酒	**sake**	rice wine
にほんしゅ・日本酒	**nihonshu**	rice wine
サイダー	**saidā**	soda
ミルクティ	**miruk tǐ**	tea with milk
トマト ジュース	**tomato jūss**	tomato juice

トニック ウォーター	**tonik uōtā**	tonic
ウイスキー	**uiskī**	whiskey
オン・ザ・ロック	**onzarok**	whiskey on the rocks
みずわり	**mizuwari**	whiskey with water
ワイン	**wain**	wine
ぶどうしゅ・葡萄酒	**budōshu**	wine

FESTIVAL FOOD

やきいも・焼き芋	**yaki-imo**	baked sweet potato
いかやき・烏賊焼	**ikayaki**	charcoal-grilled squid
わたがし・綿菓子	**watagashi**	cotton candy
たこやき・たこ焼	**takoyaki**	griddle-fried octopus
あまぐり・甘栗	**amaguri**	roasted chestnuts
とうもろこし・玉蜀黍	**tōmorokoshi**	roasted corn on the cob
おこのみやき お好み焼	**okonomiyaki**	seasoned crepe
たこせんべい 蛸煎餅	**tako sembei**	shrimp-flavored pink crackers
おでん・お田	**oden**	stew of fish and vegetable, boiled in fish broth

SHOPPING

A country *par excellence* for shopping, Japan abounds in stores of all sorts, including the ubiquitous souvenir shop. Stores generally open at 10 in the morning and stay open until late in the evening (8 or 9 PM), although department stores are usually closed after 6 PM. Japanese stores usually close for one day during the week, although many of them will be open on Sunday. If something is needed urgently then a major train station is often the place to head for. When you enter a store, sales assistants will often call out (and often quite loudly) a word of welcome, "**irash-shai-mase!**". They can rarely be expected to speak English, although writing down an English word on a piece of paper will often help.

USEFUL WORDS AND PHRASES

audio equipment	ōdio seihin
baker	pan-ya
boutique	butik
butcher	niku-ya
bookstore	hon-ya
to buy	kau
cash register	reji
CD store	shee-dee-ya
department store	depāto
fashion	fash-shon
fish market	sakana-ya
florist	hana-ya
grocer	shoku-ryō hinten
hardware store	kanamono-ya
inexpensive	yasui
menswear	shinshi fuku
newsstand	shimbun-ya
pastry shop	keiki-ya
pharmacist	kusuri-ya
receipt	ryōshū-sho

record store	rekōdo-ya
sale	sēru
shoe store	kutsu-ya
to go shopping	kaimono ni yuku
souvenir shop	omiyage-ten
special offer	tokubets kakak
to spend	okane o tskau
stationery store	bumbōgu-ya
store	mise
supermarket	sūpā
tailor	shtate-ya
toy store	omocha-ya
travel agent	ryokō-gaisha
women's wear	fujin fuku

I'd like . . .
. . . onegai-shi-mass

Do you have . . .?
. . . ari-mass ka?

How much is this?
Ikura dess ka?

Where is the . . . department?
. . . uriba wa doko dess ka?

Do you have any more of these?
Kō iu no wa mada ari-mass ka?

I'd like to change this, please
Kore o tori-kaete kure-masen ka

Have you anything less expensive?
Mō skoshi yasui no wa ari-mass ka?

Have you anything larger?
Mō skoshi ōki no wa ari-mass ka?

Have you anything smaller?
Mō skoshi chisai no wa ari-mass ka?

Does it come in other colors?
Hoka no iro mo ari-mass ka?

Could you wrap it for me?
Tsutsunde kure-masen ka?

May I have a receipt?
Ryōshū-shō kudasai?

Can I have a bag, please?
Fukuro kudasai?

May I try it (them) on?
Kite mite mo ī dess ka?

Where do I pay?
Doko de harat-tara ī dess ka?

May I have a refund?
Okane o kaeshte kudasai?

I'm just looking
Mite-iru dake dess

I'll come back later
Ato de ki-mass

THINGS YOU'LL HEAR

Irash-shai-mase!
Welcome!

Nanika osagashi dess ka?
Can I help you?

Komakai okane gozai-mass ka?
Do you have any smaller money?

Mōshi-wake gozai-masen ga ima kirashte ori-mass
I'm sorry we're out of stock

Kore dake shka gozai-masen
This is all we have

Hoka ni nanika go-iri-yō dess ka?
Will there be anything else?

Chūmon itashi-mashō ka?
Shall we order it for you?

Omochi kaeri ni nari-mass ka, otodoke shi-mashō ka?
Will you take it with you or shall we send it?

TYPES OF STORES

骨董店	**kot-tō-ten**	antique/curiosity store
パン屋	**pan-ya**	baker
本屋	**hon-ya**	bookstore
書店	**shoten**	bookstore
肉屋	**niku-ya**	butcher's
カメラ屋	**kamera-ya**	camera store

→

せともの屋	**setomono-ya**	china store
お菓子屋	**okashi-ya**	confectionery store
デパート	**depāto**	department store
クリーニング店	**kurīnin-gu-ten**	dry cleaner
電気屋	**denki-ya**	electrical goods store
両替所	**ryōgaejo**	exchange office
魚屋	**sakana-ya**	fish market
花屋	**hana-ya**	florist
果物屋	**kudamono-ya**	fruit store
八百屋	**yao-ya**	greengrocer
食料品店	**shokuryō-hin-ten**	grocery store
金物屋	**kanamono-ya**	hardware store
売店	**baiten**	kiosk
コインランドリー	**koin-randorii**	Laundromat
酒屋	**saka-ya**	liquor store
市場	**ichiba**	market
楽器店	**gak-ki-ten**	musical instrument store
めがね（店）	**megane(-ten)**	optician
ケーキ屋	**kēki-ya**	pastry shop
質屋	**shchi-ya**	pawnbroker's
薬局	**yak-kyok**	pharmacy
写真屋	**shashin-ya**	photography store
レコード店	**rekōdo-ten**	record store

→

みやげ店	**miyage-ten**	souvenir shop
スポーツ用品店	**spōts-yōhin-ten**	sporting goods store
文房具屋	**bumbōgu-ya**	stationery shop
旅行会社	**ryokō-gaisha**	travel agency

THINGS YOU'LL SEE

バーゲン	**bāgen**	bargain
大売り出し	**ō-uri-dashi**	big bargain sale
会計	**kaikei**	cashier
本日休業	**honjits kyūgyō**	closed today
割引	**waribiki**	discount
民芸品	**mingei-hin**	folk crafts
定価	**teika**	list price
名物	**meibuts**	local specialty
営業中	**eigyō-chū**	open for business
売切	**urikire**	sold out
円	**en**	yen

AT THE HAIR SALON

Hair salons by and large reflect those you find in the West, and the hairstyling vocabulary has drawn heavily on English. The Japanese service is typically more extensive, however, with extras like tea or an extended massage offered at no extra charge. Prices are not low, so no tip is required. Barbershops, **rihats-ten**, generally close on Mondays while women's hair salons, **bi-yō-in**, usually close on Tuesdays. (Note also that the first syllable of the word **bi-yō-in** should be given its full value—the slightly shorter **byōin** means "hospital"!)

USEFUL WORDS AND PHRASES

appointment	yoyak
bangs	furinj
beard	hige
blond	burondo
brush	burash
comb	kushi
conditioner	rinss
curlers	kārā
curling iron	heya-airon
curly	maki-ge
dark	kurop-poi
gel	jeru
hair	kami
haircut	sampats
hair dryer	doraiyā
hair salon	
(*beauty salon*)	bi-yō-in
(*for men*)	rihats-ten
highlights	hairaito
long	nagai
mustache	kuchi-hige
part	wakeme
perm	pāma

shampoo	shampū
to shave	hige o soru
shaving cream	hige-sori yō sek-ken
short	mijikai
styling mousse	stairin-gu mûss
wavy	uēb-shta

I'd like to make an appointment
Yoyak shtain dess

Just a trim, please
Skoshi dake kit-te kudasai

Not too much off
Amari kiranaide kudasai

A bit more off here, please
Koko, mō skoshi kit-te kudasai

I'd like a cut and blow-dry
Kat-to to burō-dorai onegai-shi-mass

I'd like a perm
Pāma kakete kudasai

I'd like highlights
Hairaito shte kudasai

THINGS YOU'LL HEAR

Dono yō ni nasai-mass ka?
How would you like it?

Kore de yoroshī dess ka?
Is that short enough?

Rinss nasai-mass ka?
Would you like any conditioner?

THINGS YOU'LL SEE

理髪店／床屋	**rihats-ten/tokoya**	barbershop
美容院	**biyōin**	beauty parlor
ビューティサロン	**byūti-saron**	beauty salon
脱色	**dash-shok**	bleach
色	**iro**	color
カット	**kat-to**	cut
調髪	**chōhats**	hair cutting
洗髪	**sempats**	hair washing
マニキュア	**manikyua**	manicure
マッサージ	**mass-sāji**	massage
パーマ	**pāma**	perm
ヘアセット	**hea-set-to**	set
シャンプーとセット	**shampū to set-to**	shampoo and set

POST OFFICES AND BANKS

Japan can boast a full and efficient postal system. Post offices
display the T̄ symbol and are open from 9 to 5 (except Sundays),
although these hours can be shortened to 9 to 3 for the post
office's banking services such as cashing international money
orders. Mailboxes are reddish-orange and, in the cities, have
two slots, the one on the left being for airmail, special delivery,
etc. Many smaller post offices are not equipped to handle
overseas packages; these can be sent from larger post offices
where customs declarations forms can also be completed. There
is a twenty-four-hour post office near Tokyo station.

Banks in Japan are open from 9 to 3 Monday to Friday and
from 9 to 12 on Saturday. All banks close on Sundays (with the
exception of one at Tokyo's Narita International Airport, which
stays open twenty-four hours a day all year round).

Remember that you'll get a better rate for traveler's checks
than for cash.

Credit cards are widely used, but the use of personal checks
is rare.

USEFUL WORDS AND PHRASES

airmail	kōkū-bin
bank	ginkō
bill (*currency*)	osats
to change	ryōgae suru
check	kogit-te
collection	shūshū
counter	madoguchi
customs form	zeikan-shinkoku-yōshi
delivery	haitats
deposit	yokin
dollar	doru
exchange rate	kawase-rēto
form	yōshi

general delivery	kyoku-dome yūbin
international money order	gaikoku-kawase
letter	tegami
letter carrier	yūbin-ya-san
list of postage rates	yūbim-butsu-ryōkin-hyō
mail	yūbim-buts
mailbox	posto
package	kozutsumi
post	yūbim-buts
postal order	yūbin-kawase
postcard	ehagaki
post office	yūbin-kyok
pound sterling	pondo
registered letter	kakitome
stamp	kit-te
surface mail	funa-bin
telegram	dempō
traveler's check	toraberāz chek
zip code	yūbim-bangō

How much is a letter to . . .?
. . . e no tegami wa ikura dess ka?

How much is a postcard to . . .?
. . . e no ehagaki wa ikura dess ka?

I would like three twenty-yen stamps
Nijū-en kit-te o sam-mai onegai-shi-mass

I want to register this letter
Kakitome de onegai-shi-mass

I want to send this package to . . .
Kono kozutsumi o . . . e okuritain dess

I want to send this to the United States
Kore o Amerika ni okuritain dess

How long does the mail to . . . take?
. . . e no yūbin wa dono kurai kakari-mass ka?

Where can I mail this?
Kore wa doko de dase-mass ka?

Is there any mail for me?
Tegami ga kite i-mass ka?

I'd like to send a telegram
Dempō uchitain dess

This is to go airmail
Kōkū-bin de onegai-shi-mass

I'd like to change this into yen
Kore o en ni kaete kure-masen ka

Can I cash these traveler's checks?
Kono toraberāz chek-ku o genkin ni shte kure-masen ka?

What is the exchange rate for the dollar?
Doru no kawase-rēto wa ikura dess ka?

THINGS YOU'LL HEAR

Paspōto, omochi dess ka?
May I see your passport, please?

Mōshi-wake gozai-masen ga . . . wa okotowari shte ori-mass
I'm afraid we don't accept . . .

THINGS YOU'LL SEE

住所	jūsho	address
あて名	atena	addressee
航空便	kōkūbin	airmail
航空書簡	kōkū shokan	airogram
銀行	ginkō	bank
記念切手	kinen kit-te	commemorative stamp
窓口	mado-guchi	counter
税関申告用紙	zeikan-shinkok-yōshi	customs declaration form
速達	sok-tats	express mail
外国為替	gaikoku kawase	foreign exchange
外国人登録証明書	gaikokujin tōrok shōmei-sho	foreign resident's ID card
用紙	yōshi	form
身分証明書	mibun shōmei-sho	ID card
手紙	tegami	letter
為替	kawase	money order
地方	chihō	out of town mail
外国向け	gaikoku-muke	overseas mail
小包	kozutsumi	package
郵便局	yūbin-kyok	post office

→

〒	yūbin-kyok no māk	post office symbol
郵便貯金	yūbin chokin	post office savings
留置	tome-oki	poste restante
印刷物	insats-buts	printed matter
現金書留封筒	genkin kakitome fūtō	registered cash envelope
書留	kaki-tome	registered mail
往復はがき	ōhuku-hagaki	return-paid postcard
船便	funabin	sea mail
切手	kit-te	stamp
普通便	futsū-bin	surface mail
電報	dempō	telegram
アメリカ向け	Amerika-muke	to America
イギリス向け	Igiriss-muke	to England
都区内	to-ku nai	to other parts of Tokyo
他府県	ta-fu ken	to other prefectures
円	en	yen

COMMUNICATIONS

Telephones: Public telephones in Japan can be found on the street, in train stations, and coffee shops. A ¥10 coin buys a one-minute local call; a ¥ 100 coin can also be used, but change is not given. Phonecards (¥1,000 and ¥500) can be purchased from machines located in various places, such as stations, airports, or by the public telephone itself, as well as from souvenir shops. You lift the receiver, insert money or a phonecard, then dial the number. The ringing tone consists of a one-second tone followed by a two-second silence; the busy tone is alternating half-seconds of tone and silence.

There are four types of public phones in Japan. Both local and long-distance calls can be made from these phones.

- The tall green phone takes ¥10 or ¥100 coins, or a phonecard. If the small red light on the phone is not lit, however, the phone accepts coins only.

- The small green phone takes a phonecard only. Both these green phones show the number of units remaining in credit (coin or phonecard), 1 unit = ¥10. when a phonecard expires, it is ejected; insert a new one to continue the call.

- The gray phone takes ¥10 or ¥100 coins, or a phonecard. there are two slots for cards; a small red light beside them indicates which slot is available. Usually they both are. The scale in the small window on the gray phone shows how much time the caller has left to speak. The procedure in the case of card expiration is the same as above.

- The pink phone is privately owned (e.g., by a coffee shop); the public may use it by inserting a ¥10 coin.

You'll find local directories in most phone booths, or you can dial 104 for Directory Assistance (which will cost ¥30).

For emergency calls dial 110 for the police and 119 for an
ambulance or the fire department. Green and gray phones
provide this service free of charge. International calls are made
through an English-speaking international operator (dial 0051),
though this can be very expensive. International direct calls
are only possible from private phones, or from public phones
with the sign "For international calls," which are usually found
in city centers, stations, and airports. The codes of three major
international telephone companies are 001, 0061, and 0041
followed by the country code. For the US, dial 001(0061 or
0041)-1 followed by the STD code minus the initial 0.

To say a phone number, just use the ordinary numerals. You
can use **no** after the area code and **ban** (which means
"number") at the end: "Tokyo 123-4567" is **Tōkyō ichi-ni-san-
no yon-go-roku-nana-ban.**

USEFUL WORDS AND PHRASES

answering machine	rusuden
call	denwa
to call	denwa suru
code	kyokuban
collect call	sempō-barai
crossed line	konsen
to dial	daiyaru suru
dial tone	daiyaru-tōn
directory assistance	an-nai
emergency	kinkyū
extension	nai-sen
international call	koksai denwa
internet	intānetto
mobile phone	keitai denwa
number	denwa-bangō
operator	kōkan-shu
payphone	kōshū denwa
phone book	denwa-chō
phonecard	terehon cādo

receiver	juwaki
telephone	denwa
telephone booth	kōshū denwa
website	web saito
wrong number	machigai denwa

Where is the nearest phone booth?
Moyori no kōshū denwa wa doko dess ka?

Is there a phone book?
Denwa-chō wa ari-mass ka?

Do you have change for the telephone?
Denwa yō no komakai okane ari-mass ka?

I would like the phone book for . . .
. . . no denwa-chō onegai-shi-mass

Can I call abroad from here?
Koko kara koksai denwa deki-mass ka?

How much is a call to . . .?
. . . e no denwa-ryō wa ikura dess ka?

I would like to make a collect call
Sempō-barai de onegai-shi-mass

I would like a number in . . .
. . . no bangō o shirabete kure-masen ka

Hello, this is . . . speaking
Moshi-moshi, kochira wa . . . dess

Is that . . .?
Sochira wa . . . dess ka?

Speaking
Hai, sō dess

I would like to speak to . . .
. . . onegai-shi-mass

Extension . . ., please
Naisen no . . . onegai-shi-mass

Please tell him . . . called
Kare ni . . . ga denwa shta to otstae kudasai-masen ka?

Ask him to call me back, please
O denwa kudasaru yō ni otstae itadake-masen ka?

My number is . . .
Watashi no denwa bangō wa . . . dess

Do you know where he is?
Kare ga doko ni irash-sharu ka gozonji dess ka?

When will he be back?
Itsu okaeri ni nari-mass ka?

Could you leave him a message?
Dengon o otstae itadake-masen ka?

I'll call back later
Ato de odenwa shi-mass

Sorry, wrong number
Sumi-masen, machigai denwa dess

How do I get an outside line?
Gaisen o tsunagitai no dess ga?

THINGS YOU'LL HEAR

Donata o oyobi dess ka?
Who would you like to speak to?

Denwa bangō ga machigat-te i-mass yo
You've got the wrong number

Donata-sama dess ka?
Who's speaking?

Moshi-moshi
Hello

Odenwa-bangō wa namban deshō ka?
What is your number?

Mōshi-wake gozai-masen ga gai-shuts chū dess
Sorry, he's not in

. . . ji ni modori-mass
He'll be back at . . . o'clock

Ashta mō ichido odenwa itadake-masen ka?
Please call again tomorrow

Odenwa ga at-ta to otstae itashi-mass
I'll tell him you called

Odenwa dess
There's a call for you

Henji ga ari-masen
There's no answer

Ohanash chū dess
The line's busy

Odenwa ga koshō dess
The phone is out of order

THINGS YOU'LL SEE

N.T.T		abbreviation of the Japan Public Telegraph & Telephone Company
電信	**denshin**	cable
電話料金	**denwa ryōkin**	call charge
電話代	**denwa-dai**	call charge
代表	**daihyō**	central switchboard
非常電話	**hijō denwa**	emergency telephone
内線	**naisen**	extension
国際電話	**koksai denwa**	international call
市内電話	**shinai denwa**	local call
長距離電話	**chōkyori denwa**	long-distance call
交換手	**kōkan-shu**	operator
市外電話	**shigai denwa**	out-of-town call
K.D.D	**koksai-denshin denwa**	Overseas Tele-communication service
電話帳	**denwa-chō**	phone book
公衆電話	**kōshū denwa**	public telephone
電報	**dempō**	telegram
電話	**denwa**	telephone
電話番号	**denwa bangō**	telephone number

HEALTH

Japan is a world leader in medicine and medical care, and in high prices, so proper medical insurance is essential. It would be wise to take along your own medications in case the medicines you are using are not available in the same form in Japan (although Western medicines are available in certain places, such as the "American Pharmacy" in central Tokyo). If possible, carry a data card showing, for instance, your blood type. For minor problems you can always go to a drugstore **yak-kyok**. For more serious problems, advice on doctors and hospitals catering to foreigners can be obtained from your embassy in Tokyo. For real emergencies memorize **isha— hayaku!** (get a doctor—quick!).

USEFUL WORDS AND PHRASES

accident	jiko
Aids	eidz
ambulance	kyūkyū sha
anemic	hinkets (no)
appendicitis	mōchō-en
appendix	mōchō
aspirin	aspirin
asthma	zensok
backache	senaka-no-itami
bandage	hōtai
(adhesive)	bando-ēdo
bite *(by dog)*	inu no kamare-kiz
(by insect)	mush-sasare
bladder	bōkō
blister	mizu-bukure
blood	ketsueki
burn *(noun)*	yakedo
cancer	gan
chest	mune
chicken pox	mizu-bōsō

cold (*noun*)	kaze
concussion	shintō
constipation	bempi
corn	uo-no-me
cough (*noun*)	seki
cut	kiri-kiz
dentist	haisha
diabetes	tōnyō-byō
diarrhea	geri
dizzy	memai
doctor	isha
earache	mimi-ita
fever	nets
filling	jūten
first aid	ōkyū te-ate
flu	ryūkan
fracture	koss-sets
German measles	fūshin
hay fever	kafum-byō
headache	zutsū
heart	shinzō
heart attack	shinzō mahi
hemorrhage	shuk-kets
hospital	byōin
ill	byōki
indigestion	shōka-furyō
injection	chūsha
itchy	kayui
kidney	jinzō
lump	kobu
measles	hashka
migraine	henzutsū
motion sickness	norimono yoi
mumps	otahuku-kaze
nausea	hakike
nurse	kangofu

operation	shujuts
optician	megane-ya
pain	itami
penicillin	penishirin
pharmacy	yak-kyok
plaster of Paris	sek-kō
pneumonia	haien
pregnant	ninshin shte-iru
prescription	shohōsen
rheumatism	ryūmachi
scald (*noun*)	yakedo
scratch	kaki-kiz
smallpox	ten-nen-tō
splinter	toge
sprain	nenza
sting	sashi-kiz
stomach	onaka
temperature (*fever*)	nets
tonsils	hentō-sen
toothache	ha-ita
ulcer	kaiyō
vaccination	yobō chūsha
to vomit	modoss, haku
whooping cough	hyakunichi-zeki

I have a pain in . . .
. . . ga itami-mass

I do not feel well
Kibun ga yoku ari-masen

I feel faint
Fura-fura shi-mass

I feel sick
Hakike ga shi-mass

I feel dizzy
Memai ga shi-mass

It hurts here
Koko ga itami-mass

It's a sharp/dull pain
Surudoku/Zuki-zuki itami-mass

It hurts all the time
Itsmo itami-mass

It only hurts now and then
Tokidoki itami-mass

It hurts when you touch it
Sawaru to itami-mass

It hurts more at night
Yoru no hō ga mot-to itami-mass

It stings
Sasu yō ni itami-mass

It aches
Itami-mass

I have a temperature
Nets ga ari-mass

I have a sore throat
Nodo ga itami-mass

I'm . . . months pregnant
Watashi wa ninshin shite . . . kagets me dess

I normally take . . .
Fudan . . . o nomi-mass

I'm allergic to . . .
. . . arerugī dess

Have you got anything for . . .?
. . . ni kiku ksuri ari-mass ka?

Can you take these if you are pregnant/breastfeeding?
Ninshin-chu/bonyū o kodomo ni agete itemo fukuyō shte
  daijōbu dess ka?

I have lost a filling
Jūten o nakshi-mashta

THINGS YOU'LL HEAR

. . . jō o nonde kudasai
Take . . . pills/tablets at a time

Mizu de
With water

Kande
Chew them

Ichi-nichi ni ik-kai/ni-kai/san-kai
Once/twice/three times a day

Neru mae ni dake
Only when you go to bed

Fudan wa nani o nomi-mass ka?
What do you normally take?

Sumi-masen, sore wa gozai-masen
I'm sorry, we don't have that

THINGS YOU'LL SEE

救急車	**kyūkyūsha**	ambulance
血液	**ketsu-eki**	blood
献血	**kenkets**	blood donation
診療所	**shinryō-jo**	clinic
診療	**shinryō**	consultation
診療時間	**shinryō-jikan**	consultation hours
歯医者	**haisha**	dentist
歯科	**shka**	dentistry
…科	**. . . ka**	. . . department
医者	**isha**	doctor
耳鼻咽喉科	**jibi-inkōka**	ear, nose, and throat department
眼科	**ganka**	eye department
病院	**byōin**	hospital
産婦人科	**sanhujinka**	obstetrics and gynecology
小児科	**shōnika**	pediatrics
赤十字	**seki jūji**	Red Cross
医院	**īn**	small hospital
外科	**geka**	surgery, operations

MINI-DICTIONARY

In this mini-dictionary you will see that some words are followed by (**no**) or (**na**). If a noun is used following such a word, then the **no** or **na** must be used:

she is pretty kanojo wa kirei dess
she is a pretty girl kanojo wa kirei na josei dess

about: about 16 jūroku kurai
accelerator akseru
accident jiko
accommodations heya
ache itami
adaptor (*electrical*) adaptā
address jūsho
admission charge nyūjō ryō
after ato
aftershave afutā-shēb-rōshon
again mata
against hantai
air conditioning eya-kon
air freshener eya-fureshnā
airline kōkū-gaisha
airplane hikōki
airport kūkō
alcohol arukōru
all zembu
  all the streets michi wa zembu
  that's all, thanks
    arigatō, sore dake dess
almost hotondo
alone hitori de
already mō
always itsmo
am: I am American Amerika-jin dess
ambulance kyūkyūsha
America Amerika

American (*person*) Amerika-jin
  (*adj.*) Amerika no
and (*with nouns*) to
  (*with verbs*) soshte
ankle ashkubi
anorak anorak
another (*different*) bets (no)
  (*further*) mō hitots (no)
answering machine rusuden
antifreeze futō-zai
antiques shop kot-tō ten
antiseptic bōfu-zai
apartment apāto
aperitif aperichif
appetite shokuyok
apple ringo
application form mōshkomi-sho
appointment yaksok
apricot anz
are: you are very kind
  anata wa totemo shinsets dess
  we are American
  watash-tachi wa Amerika-jin dess
  they are Japanese
  karera wa Nihon-jin dess
arm ude
art bijuts
art gallery bijuts-kan
artist geijuts-ka

as: as soon as possible
 dekiru dake hayak
ashtray haizara
Asia Ajia
asleep: he's asleep
 kare wa nemut-te i-mass
aspirin aspirin
at: at the post office yūbinkyoku de
 at night yoru
 at 3:00 sanji ni
attractive miryok-teki
aunt obasan
Australia Ōstoraria
Australian *(person)* Ōstoraria-jin
 (adj.) Ōstoraria no
automatic jidō
away: is it far away? tōi dess ka?
 go away! at-chi e it-te!
awful hidoi
ax ono
axle shajik

baby akachan
baby carriage uba-guruma
baby carrier akachan no kago
baby wipes bebī waipu
back *(not front)* ushiro
 (of body) senaka
backpack ryuk-sak
bacon bēkon
 bacon and eggs bēkon-eg
bad warui
baker pan-ya
balcony barukonī
ball bōru
 (dance) butō-kai
ballpoint pen bōru-pen
banana banana
band *(musicians)* bando
bandage hōtai
 (adhesive) bansōkō
bank ginkō

bar bā
 bar of chocolate itachoko
barbershop tokoya
bargain bāgen
basement chika
basket kago
bath ofuro
 to take a bath ofuro ni hairu
bathing cap sui-ei yō bōshi
bathroom ofuroba
battery denchi
beach hama
beans mame
beard hige
beautiful utskushī
because kara
 because it is too big
 ōki-sugiru kara
bed bed-do
bed linen shīts to makura-kabā
bedroom shinshits
beef gyūnik
beer bīru
before mae ni
beginner shoshin-sha
behind ushiro
beige bēju-iro (no)
bell beru
below shta
belt beruto
beside soba
best ichiban ī
better mot-to ī
between aida ni
bicycle jitensha
big ōkī
bikini bikini
bill *(currency)* osats
bird tori
birthday tanjōbi
 happy birthday! otanjōbi omedetō!
 birthday present
 tanjōbi no okurimono

bite *(verb)* kamu
  (by insect) mush-sasare
bitter *(adj.)* nigai
black kuro
blanket mōhu
blind *(cannot see)* mekura
  (on window) buraindo
blister mizu-bukure
blood ketsueki
blouse burauss
boat fune
body karada
boil *(verb: water)* wakass
  (noun: on body) hare-mono
bolt *(on door)* boruto
bone hone
book *(noun)* hon
boot būts
  (rubber) nagaguts
border kok-kyō
boring tsumaranai
born: I was born in . . .
  (place) watashi wa . . . de
  umare-mashta
  (year) watashi wa . . . nen ni
  umare-mashta
both ryōhō
  both of them futari tomo
  both of us
  watash-tachi futari
  both . . . and . . . . . . to . . . to
bottle bin
bottle opener sen-nuki
bottom *(of box, sea, etc.)* soko
bowl chawan
box hako
boy otoko no ko
boyfriend bōi-furendo
bra burajā
bracelet udewa
braces zubon-tsuri
brake *(noun)* burēki
  (verb) burēki o kakeru

brandy burandē
bread pan
breakdown *(car)* koshō
  (nervous) shinkei-suijak
breakfast chōshok
breathe iki o suru
  I can't breathe
  iki ga deki-masen
bridge hashi
briefcase kaban
British *(things)* Igiriss no
  the British Igiriss-jin
brochure panfuret-to
broil guriru
broken kowareta
  (out of order) koshō
  broken leg ashi ga oreta
brooch burōchi
brother *(older)* onīsan
  (younger) otōto
brown cha-iro (no)
bruise dabok-shō
brush *(noun)* burash
bucket bakets
Buddha Hotoke
Buddhism Buk-kyō
Buddhist *(noun)* Buk-kyō-to
  (adj.) Buk-kyō no
building tatemono
bumper bampā
burglar dorobō
burn *(verb)* moyass
  (noun) yakedo
bus bass
business shigoto
bus station bass no eki
busy *(person)* isogashī
  (crowded) konda
but demo
butcher niku-ya
butter batā
button botan
buy kau

by: **by the window** mado no soba
  by Friday kin-yōbi made ni
  by myself jibun de

cabbage kyabets
cabinet todana
cable car kēburu kā
cable TV kēbru terebi
café kiss-sa-ten
cake kēki
calculator keisan-ki
call: what's it called? nan to ī-mass ka?
camera kamera
can *(tin)* kanzume
can: can I have . . .? . . . o kure-masen ka?
Canada Kanada
Canadian *(person)* Kanada-jin
  (adj.) Kanada no
cancer gan
candle rōsok
candy ame
can opener kan-kiri
cap *(bottle)* futa
  (hat) bōshi
car kuruma
  (train) kyak-sha
carbonated tansan no
carburetor kyaburetā
card *(business)* meishi
cardigan kādigan
careful chūi-bukai
  be careful! ki o tskete!
carpet jūtan
carrot ninjin
car seat *(for a baby)* bebī shīto
cash *(money)* genkin
  (coins) komakai okane
  to pay cash genkin de harau
cassette kaset-to
cassette player tēpu rekōdā
castle oshiro
cat neko

cave hora-ana
cemetery bochi
center sentā
certificate shōmei-sho
chair iss
change *(noun: money)* otsuri
  (verb) kaeru
character *(written)* ji
check kogit-te
check *(restaurant, etc.)* okanjō
checkbook kogit-te chō
cheers! *(toast)* kampai!
cheese chīz
cherry sakurambo
chess chess
chest mune
chewing gum chūin-gam
chicken niwatori
child kodomo
children kodomo-tachi
china tōki
China Chūgok
Chinese *(person)* Chūgoku-jin
  (adj.) Chūgoku no
chocolate chokorēto
  box of chocolates hakoiri chokorēto
chop *(noun: food)* chop
  (to cut) kizamu
chopstick rest hashi-oki
chopsticks hashi
church kyōkai
cigar hamaki
cigarette tabako
city toshi
city center chūshin-gai
class kurass
classical music kurashkaru-ongak
clean kirei (na)
clear *(obvious)* meihak (na)
  (water) sumikit-ta
  is that clear?
  wakari-mass ka?
clever kashkoi

clock tokei
  (*alarm*) mezamash-dokei
close (*near*) chikai
  (*stuffy*) iki-gurushĭ
  (*verb*) shimeru
  the shop is closed
  mise wa shimat-te i-mass
clothes fuku
club kurab
  (*cards*) kurab
coat kōto
coathanger han-gā
cockroach gokiburi
coffee kōhĭ
coin -dama
  100-yen coin hyaku-en-dama
cold (*illness*) kaze
  (*weather*) samui
  (*food*) tsumetai
collar eri
collection (*stamps, etc.*) shūshū
color iro
color film karā firum
comb (*noun*) kushi
  (*verb*) tok
come kuru
  I come from . . .
  watashi wa . . . no shush-shin dess
  we came last week
  watash-tachi wa senshū ki-mashta
  come here! koko ni ki-nasai!
compartment shashits
complicated fukuzats (na)
computer komyūtā
concert ongaku-kai
conditioner (*hair*) rinss
conductor (*orchestra*) shki-sha
congratulations! omedetō!
constipation bempi
consul ryōji
consulate ryōji-kan
contact lenses kontakto renz
contraceptive hinin-yak

cook (*noun*) kok
  (*verb*) ryōri suru
cookie bisket-to
cooking utensils ryōri-dōgu
cool tsumetai
cork koruk
corkscrew koruk-nuki
corner kado
corridor rōka
cosmetics keshō-hin
cost (*verb*) kakaru
  what does it cost?
  sore wa ikura kakari-mass ka?
cotton momen
cotton balls dash-shimen
cough (*noun*) seki
cough drops nodo gsuri
country (*state*) kuni
  (*not town*) inaka
cousin itoko
crab kani
cramp keiren
crayfish zarigani
cream (*for face, food, etc.*) kurĭm
credit card kurejit-to kādo
crowded konda
cruise kōkai
crutches matsubazue
cry (*weep*) nak
  (*shout*) sakebu
cucumber kyūri
cufflinks kafuss botan
cup kap
curlers kārā
curry karē
curtain kāten
customs zeikan
cut (*noun*) kiri-kiz
  (*verb*) kiru

dad otōsan
damp shimet-ta

dance danss
dangerous abunai
dark kurai
daughter musume
day hi *see page 20*
dead shinda
deaf mimi ga tōi
dear *(person)* shtashī
  (expensive) takai
deck: deck of cards kādo hito-kumi
deck chair dek-cheya
deep fukai
deliberately wazato
dentist ha-isha
dentures ireba
deodorant deodoranto
department store depāto
departure shup-pats
develop *(film)* genzō suru
diamond *(jewel)* daiyamondo
  (cards) daiya
diaper omuts
  disposable diapers kami omutsu
diarrhea geri
diary *(record of past events)* nik-ki
  (weekly planner type) techō
dictionary jisho
die shinu
diesel dīzeru
different chigau
  I'd like a different one
  bets no ga hoshī dess
difficult muzukashī
dining car shokudō-sha
dining room shokudō
dinner yūshok
dirty kitanai
disabled karada no fujiyū (na)
dish towel fukin
dish washing liquid
  shok-ki yō senzai
distributor *(in car)* haidenki
dive tobikomu

diving board tobikomi-dai
divorced rikonshta
do suru
doctor isha
document shorui
dog inu
doll nin-gyō
dollar doru
door doa
double room *(hotel)* daburu
  (ryokan) hutari-beya
doughnut dōnats
down shta e
dress *(noun)* doress
drink *(verb)* nomu
  (noun) nomi-mono
  would you like a drink?
  nomi-mono wa ikaga dess ka?
drinking water nomi-mizu
drive *(verb)* unten-suru
driver unten-shu
driver's license untem-menkyo
driving regulations kōtsū kisok-shū
drugstore ksuri-ya
drunk yop-parai
dry kawaita
dry cleaner dorai kurīnin-gu-ya
during: during . . . . . . no aida ni
dust cloth dastā
duty-free menzei

each *(every)* sorezore
  two hundred yen each
  sorezore nihyaku en dess
early hayai
earrings iyarin-gu
ears mimi
east higashi
easy yasashī
egg tamago
either: either of them dochira demo
  either . . . or . . . . . . ka . . . ka

elastic gomu-himo
elbow hiji
electric denki no
electricity denki
electronics denshi-kōgak
elevator erebētā
else: something else
  nanika hokano mono
  someone else dareka hokano hito
  somewhere else
  dokoka hokano tokoro
email denshi meiru
email address denshi meiru no jusho
embarrassing hazukashī
embassy taish-kan
embroidery shishū
emerald emerarudo
emergency hijō
emperor ten-nō
empty kara
end owari
engaged (couple) kon-yak shta
engine (car) enjin
England Igiriss
English Igiriss no
  (language) Eigo
Englishman Igiriss-jin
Englishwoman Igiriss-jin
enlargement (photography) hikinobashi
enough jūbun
entertainment gorak
entrance iriguchi
envelope fūtō
eraser keshigom
escalator eskarētā
especially tokuni
Europe Yōrop-pa
evening yoru
every (morning, day, etc.) mai-
  (all) subete no
everyone min-na
everything min-na
everywhere doko demo

example rei
  for example tatoeba
excellent saikō
excess baggage chōka-nimots
exchange (verb) kōkan suru
exchange rate kawase sōba
excursion ensok
excuse me! shitsurei shi-mass!
  excuse me? e, nan dess ka?
exit deguchi
expensive takai
explain setsmei suru
extension (telephone) naisen
  (lengthening) kakchō
eyedrops megusuri
eye(s) me

face kao
faint (unclear) usui
  (verb) kizets suru
  to feel faint memai ga suru
fair (carnival) yūenchi
  it's not fair fukōhei dess
false teeth ireba
family kazok
fan (folding fan) senss
  (electric) sempūki
  (enthusiast) fan
fan belt fam beruto
far tōi
  how far is it . . .?
  . . . wa dono kurai tōi dess ka?
Far East Kyoktō
fare ryōkin
farm nōjō
farmer nōfu
fashion fash-son
fast hayai
fat (of person) futot-ta
  (on meat, etc.) abura
father otōsan
faucet jaguchi

fax machine fakks mashin
feel (*touch*) sawaru
  I feel hot atsui dess
  I feel like . . .
    . . . no yō na ki ga shi-mass
felt-tipped pen feruto pen
ferry ferī
fever nets
fiancé(e) kon-yak-sha
field nohara
fig ichijik
filling (*tooth*) ha no jūten
  (*of sandwich, etc.*) nakami
film (*camera*) firum
filter firutā
finger yubi
fire hi
  (*blaze*) kaji
fire extinguisher shōkaki
fireworks hanabi
first saisho (no)
first aid ōkyū teate
first floor ik-kai
first name namae
fish sakana
fishing tsuri
  to go fishing tsuri ni ik
fishing rod tsuri zao
fish market sakana-ya
flag hata
flash (*camera*) furash
flashlight kaichū dentō
flat taira (na)
flat tire pank
flavor aji
flea nomi
flight hikō
flight attendant (*female*) schūwādess
flip-flops zōri
flippers hire-ashi
flour komugi-ko
flower hana
flute furūto

fly (*verb*) tobu
  (*insect*) hae
fog kiri
folk music minzoku ongak
food tabe-mono
food poisoning shok chūdok
foot (*on body*) ashi
for: for . . . . . . no tame ni
  for me watashi no tame ni
  what for? nan no tame ni?
  for a week ish-shūkan
foreigner gaikoku-jin
forest mori
fork fōk
fortnight ni-shūkan
fountain pen man-nen-hits
fourth yombam-me
fracture zashō
free jiyū (na)
  (*no cost*) muryō
freezer reitō-ko
french fries poteto-furai
friend tomodachi
friendly shtashimi no aru
front: in front of . . .
  . . . no mae ni
frost shimo
fruit kuda-mono
fruit juice furūts jūss
fry ageru
frying pan furai pan
full ip-pai
  I'm full onaka ga ip-pai dess
full board shokuji tski
funny omoshiroi
  (*odd*) okashī
furniture kagu

garage (*parking*) shako
  (*repairs*) garēji
garbage gomi
garden niwa

garlic nin-nik
gas gasorin
gas station gasorin stando
gay (happy) yōki (na)
   (homosexual) homo (no)
gear giya
gearshift giya rebā
geisha (girl) geisha
get (fetch) mot-te kuru
   have you got . . .?
   . . . o mot-te i-mass ka?
   to get the train densha ni noru
get back: we get back tomorrow
   ashta kaeri-mass
   to get something back
   kaeshte morau
get in (to car, etc.) noru
   (arrive) tsku
get out (of bus, etc.) oriru
get up (rise) okiru
gift okurimono
gin jin
girl on-na no ko
girlfriend gārufurendo
give ageru
glad ureshī
   I'm glad ureshiku omoi-mass
glass garass
   (for drinking) gurass
glasses megane
glossy prints tsuya no aru purinto
gloves tebukuro
glue nori
go ik
   I want to go to . . .
   . . . e ikitai to omoi-mass
goggles suichū-megane
gold kin
good ī
   good! yokat-ta!
goodbye sayonara
government seifu
granddaughter mago-musume

grandfather ojīsan
grandmother obāsan
grandson mago-musko
grapes budō
grass shibafu
gray hai-iro (no)
Great Britain Igiriss
green midori-iro (no)
grocery store shoku-ryō hinten
guarantee (noun) hoshō
   (verb) hoshō suru
guidebook an-nai-sho
guitar gitā
gun (rifle) jū
   (pistol) pistoru

hair kami
haircut (for man) sampats
   (for woman) kat-to
hair dryer doraiyā
hair spray spurē
hairstylist bi-yō-in
half hambun
   half an hour sanjup-pun
half board chōshok to yūshok tski
ham ham
hamburger hambāg
hammer kanazuchi
hand te
handbag handobag
hand brake hando burēki
handkerchief hankachi
handle (door) handoru
handsome hansam (na)
hangover futska-yoi
happy shiawase (na)
harbor minato
hard katai
   (difficult) muzukashī
hard lenses (contact) hādo renz
hardware store kanamono-ya
harmony chōwa

hat bōshi
have mots
  I don't have . . .
    . . . o mot-te i-masen
  can I have . . .? . . . o kudasai?
  have you got . . .?
    . . . o mot-te i-mass ka?
  I have to go now
    ima ika-nakereba
hay fever kahum-syō
he kare
head atama
headache zutsū
headlights hed-do raito
hear kik
hearing aid hochōki
heart shinzō
heart attack shinzō mahi
heating dambō
heavy omoi
heel kakato
hello! konnichiwa!
help (noun) enjo
  (verb) taskeru
  help! taskete!
hepatitis kan-en
her: it's for her kanojo no dess
  give it to her kanojo ni agete kudasai
  her book(s) kanojo no hon
  it's hers kanojo no dess
high takai
highway kōsok-dōro
hill oka
him: it's for him kare no dess
  give it to him kare ni agete kudasai
his: his shoe(s) kare no kutsu
  it's his kare no dess
history rekshi
hitchhike hit-chi-haik
HIV positive ec-chi ai bui kansensya
hobby shumi
holiday yasumi
homeopathy dōshu ryō hō

honest shōjiki (na)
honey hachi-mits
honeymoon shinkon-ryokō
hood (car) bon-net-to
horn (car) keiteki
horrible osoroshĭ
hospital byōin
hot atsui
hot water bottle yutampo
hour jikan
house ie
how? dō?
hungry: I'm hungry
  onaka ga suite i-mass
hurry: I'm in a hurry ima isoide i-mass
husband shujin
  your husband goshujin

I watashi
ice kōri
ice cream ais-kurĭm
ice pop ais-kyandē
if moshi
ignition tenda-sōchi
ill byōki
immediately suguni
impossible fukanō
in: in Japan Nihon ni
  in Japanese Nihongo de
  in my room watashi no heya ni
India Indo
Indian (person) Indo-jin
  (adj.) Indo no
indigestion shōka-furyō
inexpensive yasui
infection kansen
information jōhō
inhaler (for asthma, etc.) kyū nyū ki
injection chūsha
injury kega
ink ink
insect mushi

insect repellent
 mush-sasare yobō-yak
insomnia fimin-shō
insurance hoken
interesting omoshiroi
internet intānetto
interpret tsūyak suru
invitation shōtai
Ireland Airurando
Irish Airurando no
Irishman Airurando-jin
Irishwoman Airurando-jin
iron (*metal*) tets
 (*for clothes*) airon
is: he/she/it is . . . kare wa/
 kanojo wa/sore wa . . . dess
island shima
it sore
itch (*noun*) kayumi
 it itches kayui dess

jacket jaket-to
jam jam
Japan Nihon
Japanese (*person*) Nihon-jin
 (*adj.*) Nihon no
 (*language*) Nihongo
Japanese-style wafū
jazz jaz
jealous shit-to-bukai
jeans jīnz
jellyfish kurage
jeweler hōseki-shō
job shigoto
jog (*verb*) jogin-gu suru
 to go for a jog jogin-gu ni dekakeru
jogging suit undō-gi
joke jōdan
just: it's just arrived chōdo tski-mashta
 I've just got one left
 hitots dake nokot-te i-mass

key kagi
kidney jinzō
kilo kiro
kilometer kiromētoru
ki___ ___ono
___) kiss
___ ___dokoro
___a
ki___hu
knit amu
know: I don't know wakari-masen
Korea Kankok
 North Korea Kita Chōsen
 South Korea Minami Chōsen
Korean (*person*) Kankoku-jin
 (*adj.*) Kankoku no

label raberu
lace rēss
lady fujin
lake mizu-umi
lamb kohitsuji
lamp stando
lampshade stando no kasa
land (*noun*) tochi
 (*verb*) chakurik suru
language gengo
large ōki
last (*final*) saigo (no)
 last week senshū
 last month sen-gets
 at last! tsui ni!
last name myōji
late: it's getting late mō osoi dess
 the bus is late
 bass wa okurete i-mass
laugh warai
Laundromat koin-randorī
laundry (*place*) sentakuya
 (*dirty clothes*) sentaku-mono
laundry detergent sentak-paudā
laxative gezai

lazy: he is lazy
  kare wa namake-mono dess
leaf ha
leaflet chirashi
learn narau
leather kawa
leave (*go away*) deru
  (*object*) nokoss
left (*not right*) hidari
  there's nothing left
  nanimo nokot-te i-masen
leg ashi
lemon remon
lemonade remonēdo
length nagasa
lens renz
less than . . . . . . yori skoshi
lesson jugyō
letter tegami
letter carrier yūbin-ya-san
lettuce retass
library tosho-kan
license menkyo
license plate nambā-purēto
life seikats
lift: could you give me a lift?
  nosete kure-masen ka?
light (*not heavy*) karui
  (*not dark*) akarui
lighter raitā
lighter fuel raitā no gass
light meter roshuts-kei
like: I like you anata ga ski dess
  I like swimming sui-ei ga ski dess
  I like it ski dess
  I don't like it ski dewa ari-masen
  it's like . . . . . . no yō dess
lime (*fruit*) yuz
line: of people rets
  (*to line up*) narabu
lip balm rip-kurīm
lipstick kuchi-beni
liqueur rikyūru

list risto
liter rit-toru
litter gomi-kuz
little (*small*) chīsai
  it's a little big skoshi ōkī dess
  just a little hon no skoshi
liver kanzō
lobster ise-ebi
lollipop ais-kyandē
long nagai
  how long does it take?
  dono kurai kakari-mass ka
long-distance bus chō-kyori bass
long-distance bus station bass no eki
lost and found wasure-mono
lot: a lot taksan
  not a lot ōku ari-masen
loud: in a loud voice ōgoe de
  (*color*) kebakebashī
lounge raunji
love (*noun*) ai
  (*verb*) ai suru
lover koibito
low hikui
luck un
  good luck! gud-do rak!
luggage tenimots
luggage rack nimots-dana
luggage room tenimotsu azukari-sho
lunch chūshok

magazine zash-shi
maid meido-san
mail (*verb*) yūsō suru
  (*noun*) yūbim-buts
mailbox yūbim-bako
make tskuru
makeup keshōhin
man hito
manager manējā
map chizu
  a map of Tokyo Tōkyō no chizu

margarine māgarin
market ichiba
marmalade māmarēdo
married: he is married
  kare wa kek-kon shte i-mass
martial arts budō
mascara maskara
mat (*straw*) tatami
match (*light*) mat-chi
  (*sports*) shiai
material (*cloth*) kiji
mattress mat-toress
maybe tabun
me: it's for me watashi no dess
  give it to me watashi ni kudasai
meal shokuji
meat nik
mechanic shūrikō
medicine ksuri
meeting kaigi
melon meron
menu menyū
message mess-sēji
middle: in the middle mannaka ni
midnight mayonaka
milk miruk
mine: it's mine watshi no dess
mineral water mineraru uōtā
minute fun
mirror kagami
mistake machigae
  I made a mistake
    machigae-mashta
mobile phone keitai denwa
modem modem
mom okāsan
monastery shūdō-in
money okane
month *see Page 21*
monument kinen-hi
moon tski
moped tansha
more mot-to

morning asa
  in the morning asa
mosaic mozaik
mosquito ka
mother okāsan
motorboat mōtā-bōto
motorcycle ōtobai
mountain yama
mouse nezumi
moustache kuchi-hige
mouth kuchi
move ugok
  don't move! ugoka-naide!
  (*house*) hik-koss
movie eiga
movie theater eiga-kan
Mr., Mrs., Ms. -san
much: not much skoshi
  much better zut-to ī dess
mug kap
museum hakubuts-kan
mushroom kinoko
music on-gak
musical instrument gak-ki
musician on-gaku-ka
mussels mūrugai
mustard karash
my: my key(s) watashi no kagi
mythology shin-wa

nail (*metal*) kugi
  (*finger*) tsume
nailfile nēru-fairu
nail polish nēru-enameru
name namae
napkin napking
narrow semai
near: near the door doa no chikak
  near Chicago
    Shikago no chikak
necessary hitsuyō
necklace nek-kuress

need (*verb*) iru
  I need . . . watashi wa . . . ga iri-mass
  there's no need to go
  iku hitsyō wa ari-masen
needle hari
negative (*photo*) nega
neither: neither of them
  dochira mo . . .-masen
  neither . . . nor . . .
  mo . . . mo . . .-masen
nephew oi
never kesh-shte
new atarashĭ
news nyūss
newspaper shimbun
newsstand shimbun-ya
New Zealand Nyūjirando
New Zealander (*person*) Nyūjirando-jin
next tsugi
  next week rai-shū
  next month rai-gets
nice steki (na)
niece mei
night yoru
nightclub naito-kurab
nightgown nemaki
no (*response*) ĭe
  I have no money okane wa ari-masen
  no sugar osatō nashide
noisy yakamashĭ
noon shōgo
north kita
Northern Ireland Kita Airurando
nose hana
not: not today kyō dewa ari-masen
  he is not here koko ni i-masen
  not for me mō kek-kō dess
  not that one sore dewa ari-masen
notebook nōto
nothing nanimo
novel shōsets
now ima
nowhere dokonimo

number sūji
nurse kangofu
nut (*fruit*) kurumi
  (*for bolt*) nat-to

occasionally tama ni
octopus tako
of no
  the name of the street
  michi no namae
office jimusho
often yok
oil sekiyu
ointment nankō
OK ok-kē
old (*thing*) furui
  (*person*) otoshiyori
olive orĭb
omelette omurets
on ue
  on the table tēburu no ue ni
  a book on Tokyo
  Tōkyō ni tsuite no hon
one (*numeral*) ichi
  (+ *noun*) hitots (no)
onion tamanegi
only dake
open (*verb*) akeru
  (*adj.*) aita
opposite: opposite the hotel
  hoteru no hantai-gawa
or soretomo
orange (*color*) orenji-iro (no)
  (*fruit*) orenji
orange juice orenj jūss
orchestra ōkestora
ordinary hutsū no
our watash-tachi no
  it's ours watash-tachi no dess
out: he's out
  kare wa gaishuts shte i-mass
outside soto

over (*more than*) ijō
  (*above*) ue
  over there mukō
oyster kaki

Pacific Ocean Taiheiyō
pacifier oshaburi
pack pak
  a pack of . . . . . . hito-hako
package (*parcel*) kozutsumi
padlock nankinjō
page pēji
pain itami
paint (*noun*) penki
pair futats (no)
  a pair of shoes kutsu iss-sok
pajamas pajama
Pakistan Pakistan
Pakistani (*person*) Pakistan-jin
  (*adj.*) Pakistan no
pale (*face*) kaoiro ga warui
  (*color*) usui
pancakes pankēki
pants zubon
pantyhose taits
paper kami
  (*newspaper*) shimbun
parents ryōshin
park (*noun*) kōen
  (*verb*) chūsha suru
parking lights saido-raito
party (*celebration*) pātī
  (*group*) dantai
  (*political*) seitō
pass (*driving*) oikoss
passenger ryokyaku
passport paspōto
path komichi
pay harau
peach momo
peanuts pīnats
pear nashi

pearl shinju
peas mame
pedestrian hokō-sha
pen pen
pencil empits
pencil sharpener empits kezuri
peninsula hantō
penpal pemparu
people hitobito
  (*nation*) kokumin
pepper koshō
  (*red/green*) pīman
peppermints hak-ka-dorop
per ni tski
  per person hitori ni tski
perfect kanzen (na)
perfume kōsui
perhaps tabun
perm pāma
petticoat pechikōto
phone book denwa-chō
phonecard terehon cādo
photocopier kopī ki
photograph (*noun*) shashin
  (*verb*) shashin o toru
photographer shashin-ka
phrase book furēzu-buk
piano piano
pickpocket suri
picnic pikunik
piece hito-kire
pier hatoba
pill jōzai
pillow makura
pilot pairot-to
pin pin
  (*clothes*) sentak-basami
pine (*tree*) mats
pineapple painap-puru
pink pink
pipe (*for smoking*) paip
  (*for water*) suidō-kan
pizza piza

place basho
plant shokubuts
plastic purass-chik
plastic bag binīru-bukuro
plate sara
platform hōm
play *(theater)* geki
pleasant kimochi no ī
please *(give me)* onegai-shi-mass
  (please do) dōzo
  please, may I take a picture:
  shashin o tot-te mo ī dess ka?
plug *(electrical)* konsento
  (sink) sen
pocket poket-to
pocketknife chīsai naifu
poison dok
police keisats
policeman omawari-san
police station keisats-sho
politics seiji
poor mazushī
  (bad quality) shits ga warui
pop music pop
pork butanik
port *(harbor)* minato
porter pōtā
  (train station) akabō
possible kanō
postcard ehagaki
poster postā
post office yūbin-kyok
potato jaga-imo
potato chips poteto-chip
poultry chōrui
pound *(British money)* pondo
powder kona
prescription shohōsen
pretty *(beautiful)* kirei (na)
  (quite) kanari
priest *(Shintō)* kan-nushi
  (Buddhist) obōsan
  (Christian) bokshi

private kojin (no)
problem mondai
  what's the problem?
  dō shi-mashta ka?
public ōyake
pull hik
purple murasaki
purse saifu
push oss
put ok

quality shits
question shitsmon
quick hayai
quiet shizuka (na)
quite *(fairly)* kanari
  (fully) suk-kari

radiator rajiētā
radio rajio
radish daikon
railroad tetsdō
rain ame
raincoat reinkōto
raisins hoshi-budō
rare *(uncommon)* mezurashī
  (steak) reya
rat dobu-nezumi
razor blades kamisori no ha
read yomu
reading lamp denki stando
  (small bedside lamp) doksho ramp
ready yōi ga deki-mashta
receipt ryōshū-sho
receptionist uketske
record *(music)* rekōdo
  (sports, etc.) kirok
record player rekōdo-prēyā
red akai
refreshments nomi-mono
refrigerator reizō-ko

registered letter kakitome-bin
relative shinrui
relax yut-tari suru
religion shūkyō
remember oboete iru
  I don't remember oboete i-masen
rent *(verb)* kass
reservation yoyak
reservation office kip-pu uriba
reserve*(verb)* yoyak suru
rest *(remainder)* sono hoka
  (relaxation) yasumu
restaurant restoran
restroom *(men's)* dansei yō toire
  (women's) fujin-toire
return *(come back)* kaeru
  (give back) kaess
rice *(uncooked)* kome
  (cooked) gohan
rich *(person)* kanemochi (no)
  (food) shits-koi
right *(correct)* tadashĭ
  (direction) migi
ring *(wedding, etc.)* yubiwa
ripe jukushta
river kawa
road michi
rock *(stone)* ishi
  (music) rok
roll *(bread)* rōru-pan
roof yane
room heya
  (space) basho
rope tsuna
rose bara
round *(circular)* marui
  it's my round watashi no ban dess
round-trip ticket ōfuku kip
rowboat bōto
rubber gom
rubber band wagomu
ruby *(stone)* rubĭ

rug *(mat)* shkimono
  (blanket) mōfu
ruins haikyo
ruler *(for drawing)* jōgi
rum ram
run *(verb)* hashiru
Russia Roshia
Russian *(person)* Roshia-jin
  (adj.) Roshia no

sad kanashĭ
safe anzen (na)
safety pin anzem-pin
sailboat hansen
salad sarada
salami sarami
sale *(at reduced prices)* sēru
salmon sake
salt oshio
same: the same people onaji hito
  same again, please
    mō hitots, onegai-shi-mass
sand suna
sandals sandaru
sand dunes sakyū
sandwich sandoich
sanitary napkins seiri-yō napkin
satellite TV sateraito terebi
sauce sōss
saucepan nabe
sauna sauna
sausage sōsēji
say iu
  what did you say? nan to ĭ-mashta
ka?
  How do you say . . . in Japanese?
    . . . wa Nihongo de dō ĭ-mass ka?
scarf skāfu
school gak-kō
scissors hasami
Scotland Skot-torando
Scottish Skot-torando no

screw neji
screwdriver neji-mawashi
scroll maki-mono
sea umi
seafood kaisem-buts
seat seki
seat belt shito-beruto
second (*adj.*) ni-bam-me (no)
  (*time*) byō
second floor ni-kai
see miru
  I can't see mie-masen
  I see (*understand*) sō dess ka
sell uru
send okuru
separate bets (no)
separated (*from husband, etc.*) wakareta
serious (*situation*) jūdai (na)
  (*person*) majime (na)
several sū-
sew nū
shampoo shampū
shave (*noun*) hige-sori
  (*verb*) hige o soru
shaving cream hige-sori-yō sek-ken
shawl shōru
she kanojo
sheet shits
shell kai
sherry sheri
Shinto (*adj.*) shintō no
Shintoism shintō
ship fune
shirt shats
shoelaces kutsu-himo
shoe polish kutsu-zumi
shoes kutsu
shopping kaimono
  to go shopping kaimono ni ik
short (*object*) mijikai
  (*person*) se ga hikui
shorts hanzubon
shoulder kata

shower (*bath*) shawā
  (*rain*) yūdachi
shower gel shawā jeru
shrimp ebi
  (*jumbo shrimp*) shiba-ebi
  (*bigger*) ise-ebi
shrine jinja
shutter (*camera*) shat-tā
  (*window*) amado
sick (*ill*) byōki
  I feel sick
  kimochi ga waruin dess
side (*edge*) hashi
  I'm on her side
  kanojo no mikata dess
sidewalk hodō
sights: the sights of . . .
  . . . no kembuts
silk kinu
silver (*color*) gin-iro (no)
  (*metal*) gin
simple kantan (na)
sing utau
single (*one*) hitots
  (*unmarried*) dok-shin
single room shinguru
sink sem-men-ki
sister (*older*) onēsan
  (*younger*) imōto
skid (*verb*) suberu
skin cleanser kurenjin-gu-kurīm
skirt skāto
sky sora
sleep (*noun*) suimin
  (*verb*) nemuru
  to go to sleep neru
sleeping bag ne-bukuro
sleeping pill suimin-yaku
slippers surip-pa
slow osoi
small chīsai
smell (*noun*) nioi
  (*verb*) niou

smile (*noun*) bishō
  (*verb*) nik-kori warau
smoke (*noun*) kemuri
  (*verb*) tabako o sū
snack keishok
snow yuki
so: so good totemo ī
  not so much . . .
  sore hodo. . . ja ari-masen
soaking solution (*for contact lenses*)
  kontakto-yō hozon-eki
soccer sak-kā
  (*soccer ball*) bōru
socks kutsu-shta
soda water sōda-sui
soft lenses softo-renz
somebody dareka
somehow nantoka-shte
something nanika
sometimes tokidoki
somewhere dokoka
son musko
song uta
soon mō sugu
sorry! gomen-nasai!
  I'm sorry sumi-masen
soup sūp
south minami
South Africa Minami Afurika
South African
  (*person*) Minami Afurika-jin
  (*adj.*) Minami Afurika no
souvenir omiyage
spade (*shovel*) ski
  (*cards*) spēdo
spare parts yobihin
spark plug tenka-purag
speak hanass
  do you speak . . .?
  . . . o hanashi-mass ka?
  I don't speak . . .
  . . . wa hanashi-masen
speed spīdo

spider kumo
spoon spūn
sprain nenza
spring (*mechanical*) bane
  (*season*) haru
stadium stajiam
staircase kaidan
stairs kaidan
stamp kit-te
stapler hoch-kiss
star hoshi
  (*movie*) stā
start shup-pats
  (*verb*) shup-pats suru
station eki
statue dōzō
steak stēki
steal nusumu
  it's been stolen nusumare-mashta
stockings stok-kin-gu
stomach onaka
stomachache fuku-tsū
stop (*verb*) tomaru
  (*bus stop*) bass-tei
  stop! tomare!
store mise
storm arashi
strawberry ichigo
stream ogawa
street tōri
string (*cord*) himo
  (*guitar, etc.*) gen
stroller uba-guruma
student gaksei
stupid baka
suburbs kōgai
subway chikatets
sugar osatō
suit (*noun*) sūts
  (*verb*) au
  it suits you anata ni ai-mass
suitcase sūts-kēss
sun taiyō

sunbathe nik-kō-yok
sunburn hiyake
sunglasses sangurass
sunny: it's sunny hi ga dete i-mass
suntan hiyake
suntan lotion hiyake rōshon
supermarket sūpā
supplement (*for fares*) tsuika-kin
sweat (*noun*) ase
　(*verb*) ase o kak
sweater jampā
sweatshirt undō-sētā
sweet amai
swimming pool pūru
swimming trunks kaisui-pants
swimsuit kaisui-gi
switch sui-chi

table tēburu
taillights tēru-ramp
Taiwan Taiwan
take toru
　can I take it with me?
　mot-te it-te mo ī dess ka?
　take a picture!
　shashin o tot-te!
　I'll take a taxi takshī de iki-mass
takeoff ririk
takeout mochi-kaeri
talcum powder tarukamu-paudā
talk (*noun*) hanashi
　(*verb*) hanass
tall takai
tampon tampon
tangerine mikan
tape (*invisible, adhesive*) serotēp
tapestry tapestorī
taxi takshī
tea (*Western*) kōcha
　(*Japanese*) ocha
teahouse chamise
team chīm
telegram dempō

telephone (*noun*) denwa
　(*verb*) denwa suru
telephone booth denwa boks
telephone call denwa
television terebi
temperature ondo
　(*fever*) nets
temple otera
tent tento
than yori
thank (*verb*) kansha suru
　thanks arigatō
　thank you dōmo arigatō
that: that bus ano bass
　what's that? are wa nan dess ka?
　I think that . . . . . . to omoi-mass
their: their room(s) karera no heya
　it's theirs karera no dess
them: it's them karera dess
　it's for them karera no dess
　give it to them karera ni age-nasai
then sore kara
there (*near you*) soko
　(*over there*) asoko
　there is/are . . . . . . ari-mass
　there isn't/aren't . . . . . . ari-masen
　is there . . .? . . . ari-mass ka?
thermos® mahō-bin
these: these things kono mono
　these are mine
　korera wa watashi no dess
they karera
thick atsui
thin usui
thing (*abstact*) koto
　(*concrete*) mono
think omou
　I think so sō omoi-mass
　I'll think about it
　kangaete mi-mass
third sambam-me
thirsty: I'm thirsty
　nodo ga kawaite i-mass

this: this bus kono bass
  what's this? kore wa nan dess ka?
  this is Mr. . . . .
  kochira wa . . .-san dess
those: those things sono mono
  those are his
  sorera wa kare no dess
throat nodo
through: through Tokyo Tōkyō keiyu
thumbtack oshi pin
thunderstorm raiu
ticket kip
tie (noun) nek-tai
  (verb) musubu
time jikan
  what's the time?
  ima nanji dess ka?
timetable jikok-hyō
tip (money) chip
  (end) saki
tire (on wheel) taiya
tired tskareta
  I feel tired tskare-mashta
tissues tish-shū-pēpā, tissyū
to: to America Amerika e
  to the station eki e
  to the doctor oisha-san e
toast tōsto
tobacco tabako
today kyō
toe ashi no yubi
together ish-sho ni
toilet otearai
toilet paper toiret-to pēpā
tomato tomato
tomato juice tomato jūss
tomorrow ashta
tongue shta
tonic tonik
tonight kon-ya
too (also) mo
  (excessive) -sugiru
tooth ha

toothache: I have a toothache
  ha ga itain dess
toothbrush ha-burash
toothpaste ha-migaki
tour ryokō
tourist ryokō-sha
towel taoru
tower tawā
town machi
town hall shiyak-sho
toy omocha
tractor toraktā
tradition dentō
traffic kōtsū
traffic jam kōtsū-jūtai
traffic lights shingō
trailer (for car) torērā
train densha
translate hon-yak suru
transmission (for car) toransmishon
trash can gomibako
travel agency ryokō-gaisha
traveler's check toraberāz-chek
tray obon
tree ki
trip (journey) ryokō
truck torak
trunk (car) torank
try yat-te miru
tunnel ton-neru
turn signal winkā
tweezers pinset-to
typewriter taipuraitā

umbrella kasa
uncle ojisan
under shta
undershirt chok-ki
underwear pants
university daigak
until made
unusual mezurashī

125

up ue
  (upward) ue made
urgent kyū (na)
us: it's for us
  watash-tachi no dess
  give it to us
  watash-tachi ni kudasai
use *(noun)* shiyō
  (verb) tskau
  it's no use
  yaku-ni tachi-masen
useful yaku-ni tats
usual itsmo no
usually itsmo

vacancy *(room)* aki-beya
vacuum cleaner sōjiki
valley tani
valve ben
vanilla banira
vase kabin
veal ko-ushi no nik
vegetable yasai
vegetarian saishok-shugi-sha
vehicle kuruma
very totemo
  very much totemo
video tape bideo tēpu
view: a good view i nagame
viewfinder fainda
villa bess-sō
village mura
vinegar su
violin baiorin
visa biza
visit *(noun)* hōmon
  (verb) hōmon suru
visitor hōmon-sha
  (tourist) ryokō-sha
vitamin pill bitamin-zai
vodka uok-kā
voice koe

wait mats
waiter uētā
  waiter! sumi-masen!
waiting room machi-ai-shits
waitress uētoress
Wales Uēruz
walk *(noun: stroll)* sampo
  (verb) sampo suru
  to go for a walk sampo ni ik
wall kabe
wallet saifu
war sensō
wardrobe yōfuku-danss
warm atatakai
was: I was watashi wa . . . deshta
  he was kare wa . . . deshta
  she was kanojo wa . . . deshta
  it was sore wa . . . deshta
wasp suzume-bachi
watch *(noun)* tokei
  (verb) miru
water mizu
waterfall taki
wave *(noun)* nami
  (verb) te o furu
we watash-tachi
weather tenki
website web saito
wedding kek-kon-shki
week shū *see page 21*
Welsh Uēruz (no)
were: we were
  watash-tachi wa . . . deshta
  you were anata wa . . . deshta
  (sing. familiar) kimi wa . . . deshta
  they were
  karera wa . . .deshta
west nishi
  the West seiyō
Westerner seiyō-jin
Western-style yōfū
wet nureta
what? nani?

wheel (*of bicycle*) sharin
  (*steering*) handoru
wheelchair kuruma-iss
when? its?
where? doko?
which? (*of two*) dochira?
  (*of more than two*) dore?
whiskey uiskī
white shiroi
who? dare?
why? naze?
wide hiroi
wife tsuma
  my wife kanai
  your wife oksan
wind kaze
window mado
windshield uindo-skrīn
wine budōshu
wine list wain-risto
wing tsubasa
with (*together with*) to ish-sho ni
  I'll go with you
  a nata to ish-sho ni iki-mass
  (*using*) de
  with a pen pen de
  with sugar satō iri
without nashide
  without sugar satō nashide
woman josei
wood mori
wool yōmō
word kotoba
work (*noun*) shigoto
  (*verb*) hatarak
  it doesn't work ugoki-masen

worse mot-to warui
worst ichiban warui
wrapping paper tsutsumi-gami
wrench spana
wrist te-kubi
write kak
writing paper binsen
wrong: it is wrong machigat-te i-mass

year see page 21
yellow kiroi
yen en
yes hai
yesterday kinō
yet mō
  not yet mada
yogurt yōhuruto
you (*sing. polite*) anata
  (*sing. familiar*) kimi
  (*plural polite*) anata-gata
  (*plural familiar*) kimi-tachi
your: your shoe(s)
  (*polite*) anata no kutsu
  (*familiar*) kimi no kutsu
yours: is this yours? (*polite*)
  kore wa anata no dess ka?
  (*familiar*) kore, kimi no?
youth hostel yūss hosteru

zen zen
zen Buddhism zen-shū
zen garden zendera no niwa
zipper chak
zoo dōbutsu-en

DK Eyewitness Travel Guides titles include:
Amsterdam · Australia · Sydney · Berlin · Budapest · California
Florida · Hawaii · New York · San Francisco & Northern California
Canada · France · Loire Valley · Paris · Provence · Great Britain
London · Ireland · Dublin · Scotland · Greece: Athens & the Mainland
The Greek Islands · Istanbul · Italy · Florence & Tuscany
Milan & the Lakes · Naples · Rome · Sardinia · Sicily
Venice & the Veneto · Jerusalem & the Holy Land · Mexico · Moscow
St. Petersburg · Portugal · Lisbon · Prague · South Africa
Spain · Barcelona · Madrid · Seville & Andalusia · Thailand
Vienna · Warsaw